HACKING THE FUTURE

HACKING
THE
FUTURE

PRIVACY, IDENTITY, AND
ANONYMITY ON THE WEB

COLE STRYKER

Overlook Duckworth
New York • London

This edition first published in hardcover in the United States and the
United Kingdom in 2012 by Overlook Duckworth, Peter Mayer Publishers, Inc.

NEW YORK
141 Wooster Street
New York, NY 10012
www.overlookpress.com
For bulk and special sales, please contact sales@overlookny.com

LONDON
90-93 Cowcross Street
London EC1M 6BF
inquiries@duckworth-publishers.co.uk
www.ducknet.co.uk

Cataloguing-in-Publication Data is available from the Library of Congress.

Design and typeformatting by Bernard Schleifer
Manufactured in the United States of America
3 5 7 9 10 8 6 4 2

ISBN US: 978-1-59020-974-5
ISBN UK: 978-0-7156-4404-1

Contents

*For the uncelebrated, often anonymous geniuses—
the phreaks, geeks, hackers, crackers and punks.
You charted the course of the Internet, through
neither force nor fiat, but by the thrust of your wild,
uncompromising imaginations. You created, and the rest
of the world saw that it was good. With unparalleled
passion and foresight, you made the Internet the
potent tool for individual freedom and self
expression it has become. Thank you.*

ACKNOWLEDGMENTS

Many thanks to the team at Overlook Press, especially my wonderful editor Stephanie Gorton, publicist Michael Goldsmith, and president Peter Mayer, whose enthusiasm for my work has made for another invigorating writing experience. Thanks to my super agent, Chelsea Lindman, the incredibly smart and sweet Amber Baker, B. Michael Payne, Chris Menning, and Whitney Phillips for their insight, readiness to help, and encouraging GIFs.

Lastly, thanks to all the people who agreed to contribute an interview, anonymous or otherwise.

"Man is least himself when he talks in his own person. Give him a mask, and he will tell you the truth."
—OSCAR WILDE

Introduction

I think anonymity on the Internet has to go away. People behave a lot better when they have their real names down. . . . I think people hide behind anonymity and they feel like they can say whatever they want behind closed doors.

In July 2011, Randi Zuckerberg, then marketing director of Facebook, uttered the words above during a panel discussion hosted by *Marie Claire* magazine. She couldn't have anticipated the firestorm those few words would generate among those already uncomfortable with the direction the Web had taken in the preceding year.

Two years prior, Google CEO Eric Schmidt, in an interview with CNBC's Maria Bartiromo, gave the downright schoolmarmish advice, "If you have something that you don't want anyone to know, maybe you shouldn't be doing it in the first place." Schmidt, who once led an antitrust crusade against Microsoft, has claimed that Google will avoid Microsoft's missteps because the search giant faces compelling incentives to please a customer base that will seek services elsewhere the moment Google does anything shady. But what if Google's been tracking your search results for your entire life? Google, just one of dozens of companies that mines user data, knows your favorite foods, your sexual proclivities, and your medical history, to say nothing of the personal information they host in the form of e-mails and other documents. Would it be as simple as just walking away?

Before the Internet Age, computers were perceived by the public as unfeeling, literally *calculating* metal boxes that just might help bring about a nuclear apocalypse. As machines go, they were just as cold as their industrial-era forebears, if not more so—at least you can watch the parts move on a steam engine. At least you knew it wasn't somehow plotting against you. It wasn't so long ago that computers were seen as a dehumanizing tool of a dystopic new technocracy, imbued with the fear and existential despair brought by the Cold War's lingering sense of impending doom.

But then something changed. Today we see computers (we don't even really call them that anymore, they're mobiles or laptops or something that sounds friendlier) as being vital, almost countercultural gadgets that bring empowered individualism, collaborative communities, and, depending on whom you ask, an almost spiritual enlightenment. They're sleek and sexy. They're our salvation from a world of physical limitations and disparities. Computers help us learn, work, and connect—Facebook now claims 850 million members, a figure that eclipses the number of people who were online in 2004. Pop stars interface with tween girls on devices with names like "Razr Maxx." How did we get here? How did these calculators, manipulated by flat-topped military brainiacs in austere labs, become something so integral to the human experience that to call them an extension of the self hardly seems like an overstatement?

Surely part of the answer is technological. We all know the first computers filled entire rooms in order to accomplish the computational tasks that you can now do (gee whiz!) in the palm of your hand. Another part of the transformation has to do with design evolution of machines. An iPad is certainly much sexier than bland, beige computers that existed even a decade ago.

But more than style, cost, and convenience, more than any other factor, the simple act of linking one computer to another brought about a new stage of human social evolution, the most rapid and far-reaching in human history with the possible exception of the printing press. And it happened because a bunch of geeks in California, Massachusetts, and elsewhere in the country picked up where the military-industrial complex left off after the Cold War.

The Internet could have never been born of state decree. It's too dangerous. It's too difficult to monitor and control. It's far too unwieldy. No, something so decentralized, open, and free could only have been conceived in an environment embodying those characteristics. The military had designed a decentralized computer network equipped with routing and packet switching because they wanted the system to survive if one of its nodes was located in a city that was nuked. This open platform enabled geeks to tinker in their basements and surreptitiously fiddle with pay phones while they made fascinating new discoveries about how communications systems worked, and how they could overcome the restrictions around those systems.

Throughout the '80s we saw something truly magical, the

formation of the first ad hoc virtual communities—Bulletin Board Systems. It wasn't cheap, but with the right tools and know-how, anyone could set up a BBS and start up a little nation-state that played by his rules, and if the members of the BBS didn't like it, they could go somewhere else, or start their own. It was an opportunity for people to become "as gods," in the words of Web pioneer Stewart Brand, in control of their own identities, and thus their destinies, like never before. You could be gay on the Internet and nobody could do a thing about it. You could pretend you were a cat. You could be a prince online, whether rich or poor in reality. Now we're getting to the crux of it.

Computer technology has changed many things, but the most profound has been the ability to empower individuals to redefine themselves in a social environment, to hack into their personhood, their identity, and truly become who they want to be. It doesn't matter if you're ugly or physically disabled—no one needs to know. And that freedom is contingent on the ability of Web users to take control of their identities—to be as anonymous or pseudonymous as they want to be.

At least, that was how it was *supposed* to work.

As the Web has developed since the '80s, it's become more lucrative for people who want to sell you things. And it follows that it's become more lucrative to become the kind of politician who pushes for regulation of the Internet so that people who want to sell you things can do so more efficiently. Meanwhile, the rise of social networks has been accompanied by an unsettling accumulation of private information, given over to corporations willingly by those who wish to seamlessly engage with the Web.

At the same time, a global network of pranksters, activists, and bullies, drawing from two decades of privacy and free-speech activism, have taken on the anti-persona of "Anonymous," donning masks and causing havoc ranging from picking on classmates to bringing down the Web sites of multinational corporations. These (mostly) smart, well-connected people from a seemingly infinite range of backgrounds and an equally diverse set of motivations see anonymity as a source of power, perhaps the most integral human liberty that can be provided in a free society. They're loosely organized, and they often clash within the group. But their amateurish disorganization mirrors the early Internet in that there's no primary control center, no head to decapitate. Similarly, the folks behind WikiLeaks have taken up the fight against control of the Web from a different angle. They're less chaotic, and thus more approachable to the media. They at least operate under the pretense of working within the law, but the threat they pose to the establishment is equally grave. Where their fathers hacked machines, these freedom-loving network natives are hacking the media, politics, and, most important, the self, in dynamic and unpredictable ways.

It made sense that the Internet would become a battleground between the haves and have-nots, with information as currency, whether personal or political. What we've seen in 2010 and 2011 is that the Internet isn't quite as locked-down as power brokers thought, and people weren't going to give up control of the open Internet without a fight.

That the Internet evolved the way it did almost seems like an accident. It spilled throughout the globe. In many ways it upends traditional power structures, encourages unlikely alliances, and spreads knowledge and hope for a better world. Governments and corporations may be able to sway the gavel, the sword, the coin, but the individual controls the wires, wrangling technology to conduct asymmetrical warfare, continuously evolving new ways to wrest control from the historically powerful.

The Web will continue to see warfare in the coming decade. Its primary battleground will be the identity space. Your ability to define who you are as a human, to be as open or as private with your personal information as you want to be, to speak out against injustices anonymously, or to role-play as someone you wish you were—these are the freedoms we will fight to keep. Will you decide who you are or will you be defined by the identity brokers?

On the face of it, we recognize cyberbullying, child pornograpy distribution, faceless slander, and data theft to be universally recognized evils, and we should therefore do what we can to mitigate them. The simple, obvious solution is to force everyone to wear a name tag in cyberspace, so that everyone is responsible for their actions online, just like in the real world. Evildoers use anonymity as both a shield and a weapon. If we rob them of both, we'll have less evil.

My position: It's just not that simple. Throughout *Hacking the Future* I trace the rich heritage of anonymous speech in a free society and examine its most popular current manifestations. I explore the bits and bytes behind the argument. I use the technology and come face-to-face with unspeakable evils in dark places I'd prefer never to return to. I consult the men who shaped the Internet and the soldiers toiling in the trenches of network security who intimately recognize the terrifying potential of the Wild Wild Web daily. I talk to code breakers, whistle-blowers, researchers, hacktivists, and mothers.

This book is essentially a long form rebuttal to Ms. Zuckerberg's comments. Her attitude is shared by many within the tech industry, and even more outside that universe. I wanted to figure out if it's worth living with anonymity on the Internet because I believe, without a doubt, that the Internet is the most important tool we have for promoting liberty. The identity issue may be the most crucial decision we face in the coming decade.

The Web is being pulled in two directions. In the worst fears of free-speech advocates, the Internet becomes tightly regulated and real-name identities are enforced, such that everything you say can be traced back to you. The reverse dystopia is a lawless frontier, where cyberterrorists, pedophiles, and information thieves run free. The decisions that lawmakers and CEOs make today regarding the privacy of Internet users will determine the way the Web looks in the future. As the "real world" and cyberspace become increasingly intertwined, society has yet to determine if it wants the Web to be an electronic extension of one's off-line life or something entirely different.

1

A Brief History of Anonymity

How dreary to be somebody!
How public, like a frog
To tell your name the livelong day
To an admiring bog!
—Emily Dickinson

BEFORE THE development of the printing press and the resultant publishing industry, attribution was the exception to the rule. The oral tradition held no copyright—folk stories and music belonged to everyone. In most cases, no one cared about securing a reputation benefit because artistic works were passed around memetically across societies. The most prolific creator in human experience, in every artistic field, was and is Anonymous. But even after the age of recorded media had begun, many dramatists, satirists, composers, and activists held on to their anonymity for one reason or another. Many of our most beloved works were published anonymously, and it wasn't until much later that the identities of their authors were discovered. *Pride and Prejudice. Frankenstein. Robinson Crusoe.*

To Uphold Modesty

You may not have heard of Charles Lutwidge Dodgson, but you're probably familiar with his *Alice in Wonderland* series, which he published under the pen name Lewis Carroll. Dodgson was a painfully shy man and valued his personal privacy above the glory of having written one of the most beloved children's stories of all time. He begged friends not to reveal the connection between his Christian name and Lewis Carroll as the latter's renown grew. Dodgson published several textbooks under his own name, but the stories he published as Carroll were "for fun."

In many cases this modesty was often driven by a sense of duty to God. To reveal one's authorship was often seen throughout history as an egotistical, self-gratifying exercise. In some cultures it was considered ungentlemanly for a man to publish under his own name. Throughout history, works of confession have brought solace to reformed evildoers, but to detail one's indiscretions was considered, to borrow a phrase from the blogging era, "oversharey." John Newton, the man responsible for the most universally recognized Christian hymn, "Amazing Grace," also wrote *An Authentic Narrative of Some Remarkable and Interesting Particulars in the Life of* ******** in 1764. He was anxious about focusing on "the Self" and took pains to keep the focus of his works on the redemptive power of Christ rather than on his own seedy exploits, including involvement with the slave trade, sexual abandon, and assorted blasphemies.

To Stymie Sexists

For many years, works penned by women were pseudonymous by default. They would most often have their work attributed as "By a Lady." Perhaps the most legendary female
author ever, Jane Austen, originally used this pseudonym.
There are many examples of women taking on a male moniker
to avoid ad hominem criticism, forcing critics to focus on the
works themselves rather than the author. Charlotte Brontë
wrote the following to one of her harshest critics, George
Henry Lewes, in 1849:

> To such critics I would say, "To you I am neither man nor
> woman—I come before you as an author only. It is the sole
> standard by which you have a right to judge me—the sole
> ground on which I accept your judgment."

Long before Mary Ann Evans achieved literary success for
works such as *Silas Marner* and *Middlemarch*, she wrote *Scenes
of a Clerical Life*, her first published fictional work. She wrote
it under the nom de plume George Eliot, which allowed her
to captivate readers with her depiction of the lives of a trio of
reverends, written in the authoritative voice of a clergyman. It
is likely that had Evans published under her given name, her
work would have been lambasted by critics. After all, what
could a woman know of the clerical life? To put on manhood
was to put on authority. Her pseudonym exempted readers
from struggling with cultural prejudices that may have kept
them from enjoying the work for itself.

> For several reasons I am very anxious to retain my incognito
> for some time to come, and to an author not already famous
> anonymity is the highest prestige. Besides if George Eliot turns

out a dull dog and an ineffective writer—a mere flash in the pan—I for one am determined to cut him on the first intimation of that disagreeable fact.

To Elude the Noose

The history of publishing in the West is rife with authors being persecuted for writing, printing, and distributing literature that challenges the political status quo, be it political power, social norms, or economic conditions.

In 1532 François Rabelais began writing his *Great and Inestimable Chronicles of the Grand and Enormous Giant Gargantua*. They were deemed not only obscene but heretical by the University of Paris. Étienne Dolet, a friend of Rabelais's, had been hanged for publishing a platonic dialogue that denied the existence of the immortal soul.

Meanwhile in England, monarchs had good reason to fear anonymity. In 1538, the first licensing law was introduced, which required all books to be approved by a royal nominee. This attitude toward anonymous publication was reiterated throughout the ages, with Henry VIII proclaiming in 1546 that printers must include their name, the name of the author, and the date of printing on every book. Edward VI later issued a similar proclamation to stifle any kind of reading beyond the Scriptures (and of course, some translations of the Scriptures were taboo). Elizabeth I reinforced the policy, specifically targeting Catholic works.

In 1579, John Stubbs's hand was cut off following the publication of *The Discovery of a Gaping Gulf Whereinto England Is Like to Be Swallowed by Another French Marriage*, a scathing denunciation of Elizabeth I's betrothal to Francis, Duke of Anjou. Ten years later, "Martin Marprelate" mocked the Church of England and even named names, cheerfully lobbing Molotov cocktails of searing wit at authority figures. It was one of the first examples of an author who used anonymity proactively and not simply for self-defense.

Monarchs continued to decree laws prohibiting anonymous publication in 1643 with the Ordinance for the Regulation of Printing, in 1660 with the Treason Act, and the Printing Act of 1662. The pioneering activists who raged against these laws helped to soften society's reaction to public insult. In seventeenth-century England, insulting a peer would often lead to a duel, and to offend a social superior would lead to beating or imprisonment.

The danger in publishing was not limited to the author. In 1663, London printer John Twyn's head was placed on a spike and displayed over Ludgate. His body was quartered, and each section was sent to four other city gates. His crime? Printing an anonymous pamphlet entitled *A Treatise of the Execution of Justice*, which declared that monarchs should be accountable to their subjects and affirmed their right to rebel against unjust rulers. Twyn insisted that he did not even know the name of the author, but even if he had, he would refuse to give up his name. Printers who declared they hadn't even read a work could not claim immunity. The crown needed a scapegoat, and if they couldn't pin down the author of an incendiary work, the printer, or even the bookbinder, would have to do.

In 1682 John Locke published *Two Treatises of Government*, one of the most influential works of political philosophy, paving the way for the democratic revolution that would sweep the Western world in the coming centuries. *Two Treatises* argued that a monarch's duty was to his subjects and that his rule was given to him by the people, not by divine right. But the work wasn't always attributed to Locke. In fact, Locke was incredibly paranoid that he would be found out and swore his close friends to secrecy. Locke's work was held in high esteem by American revolutionaries, along with another work, written by John Trenchard and Thomas Gordon under the pseudonym "Cato." *Cato's Letters*, first appearing in 1720, influenced the thinking of Benjamin Franklin, Thomas Jefferson, and John Adams, among others.

To Make Mischief

Some authors concealed their identities for much the same reason that members of Anonymous do today. They were trolls, bent on upsetting the equilibrium of the established social, political, or ecclesiastical order, and anonymity both protected and liberated them. Consider Jonathan Swift, a man who went to tremendous lengths to ensure the anonymous publication of *Gulliver's Travels* in 1726. He arranged for an intermediary to hand off the manuscript to a publisher. Gulliver's adventures among the Lilliputians, the Houyhnhnms, and the Yahoos, viciously parodying the pious and pompous of his day, are considered among the greatest works of satire. The book's release inspired a frenzy of speculation about the author, which fueled sales. The book has never been out of print. In "A Modest Proposal," also published anonymously, Swift again skewered the social scene of his day, going so far as to humorously suggest that the poor children of Ireland should be served as food to their parents in order to deal with country's rampant poverty.

Seven years later, Alexander Pope published *An Essay on Man* anonymously. Leonard Welsted, one of Pope's literary rivals who'd often publicly mocked his works, praised *An Essay on Man* as "above all commendation." Pope later had Welsted's praise published and ridiculed accordingly.

But even as the public appetite for satire increased and content restrictions diminished, anonymous publication continued. In the late nineteenth century, Samuel Butler published several satirical works anonymously because he was the son of a clergyman and was concerned that his family would disapprove of his writings.

A century later, an anonymous work called *Primary Colors*, published in 1996, would send shock waves throughout Bill Clinton's presidential administration. It was publicized on the dust jacket as "the kind of truth that only fiction can tell." The media rabidly attempted to track down the author. The *Washington Post* obtained an early draft of the novel, complete with handwritten notes, and commissioned a handwriting analysis, which matched the pen to journalist Joe Klein, who was subsequently excoriated by fellow journalists and forced to resign.

The Triumph of Anonymity

In 1734 John Peter Zenger was arrested in the United States for publishing pseudonymous essays attacking New York governor William Cosby. Defending Zenger in court, his lawyer pleaded the jury to lay "a foundation for securing to ourselves, our posterity, and our neighbors" the right of "exposing and opposing arbitrary power . . . by speaking and writing truth." The jury acquitted Zenger in a landmark case that established protections for American writers under British common law, a remarkable legal evolution that paved the way for a broader freedom of the press.

This ruling allowed Thomas Paine to publish "Common Sense" in 1776 under the name "An Englishman." Other writers wrote under pen names like "A Pennsylvanian," "A Friend to the Liberty of His Country," or "A Federal Farmer." Most famously, Alexander Hamilton, John Jay, James Madison, Samuel Adams, and others created the "Federalist Papers" under the name "Publius." These pseudonymous works were powerful—essential, even—in shaping the democracy that was to come.

Once democracy had been secured, anonymity would be used to fight for other goals, like civil rights and women's rights. The *National Association for the Advancement of Colored People (NAACP) v. Alabama* case was a watershed moment for anonymity rights. The state of Alabama filed a lawsuit and attempted to subpoena the organization to force it to disclose its full membership list. The NAACP successfully proved that previous disclosure of its membership had resulted in "economic reprisal, loss of employment, threat of physical coercion, and other manifestations of public hostility." Alabama argued that because these offenses were not related to state action, but of private citizens, the First Amendment did not apply. The court disagreed, noting that the state action was directly correlated with abuses committed by private actors. In the end the court recognized, "Inviolability of privacy in group association may in many circumstances be indispensable to preservation of freedom of association, particularly where a group espouses dissident beliefs."

In 1960 the right to distribute pamphlets anonymously was called into question in *Talley v. California*. Talley had been convicted and fined in Los Angeles because he was distributing handbills that did not carry "the name of the individual who caused it to be distributed."

We have recently had occasion to hold in two cases that there are times and circumstances when States may not compel members of groups engaged in the dissemination of ideas to be publicly identified. . . . The reason for those holdings was that identification and fear of reprisal might deter perfectly peaceful discussions of public matters of importance.

Twenty-five years later came the commercial Internet, a relatively free and open platform that promised creators and activists a way to communicate their ideas unencumbered not only by publication and distribution costs but also the meddlesome hands of the state. Anonymity was, for the most part, hardwired into the very protocols that serve as the foundation for the global computer network. Information was sent and received through packets, and when a packet arrives at your end of the connection, it doesn't explicitly have to tell you where it came from.

One of the first methods conceived to allow people to communicate anonymously was the remailer. An anonymous remailer privatizes e-mail correspondence, allowing users to send messages to individuals or entire Usenet groups without revealing the identity of the sender (Usenet was a popular Web community in the '80s that functioned like a hybrid between a message board and e-mail). There are a few different kinds. Some remailers strip the address of the sender completely and keep no logs. The Mixmaster remailer, developed by Lance Cottrell, uses a program to mix up packets of information, like puzzle pieces, and then reorders the packets upon receipt.

I spoke with Cottrell about his experience developing the Mixmaster remailer.

The first remailers were pretty crude. People added encryption to them, and I ran some. Everyone was talking about the vulnerabilities, so I built a remailer that would be much more difficult to attack. I built the first version, got some feedback, and then built the 2.0 version, which really caught on. This was all just in my spare time. We'd all been talking about it but no one had built a tool.

Cottrell's remailer fixed a crucial vulnerability. Remailers were designed to send a message through multiple hubs. Because of the way cryptography works, each layer of encryption adds extra size to the message. If a fully encrypted message with all three layers is 100k, and each layer adds 1k of space to the message, I can connect the pathway across the hubs just by correlating the size that's knocked off at each hub. For example, let's say I want to send an e-mail to you. I encrypt it with the key of the last remailer I want it to go to. And then I put on a message to deliver to remailer 3, and I encrypt it with remailer 2's key. And then I attach a message that says, "Send this to remailer 2," and I encrypt it with remailer 1's key, then I send it to remailer 1. So remailer 1 gets it, decrypts it, sends it to 2, 2 decrypts it, sends it to 3, and 3 decrypts it and delivers it to the recipient.

The most famous anonymous remailer was anon.penet.fi, developed by Johan Helsingius in Finland, which operated from 1993 to 1996. At the time, administrators of university networks argued about whether or not everyone participating in the network should voluntarily put their proper name on messages so that everyone would be held accountable. Helsingius argued, as techies are wont to do, that "the Internet just doesn't work that way . . . and if somebody actually tries to enforce that, the Internet will always find a solution around it." To prove his point, Helsingius kept the anonymous remailer running, to prove that there is always a technological solution to circumvent censorship. "It was a question of control. . . . I think that's one of the strengths of the network, that nobody can control it."

Helsingius may have been a bit too optimistic. In 1995, Finnish police shut down anon.penet.fi, which was used, among other things, to distribute internal documents published by the Church of Scientology. As far as enemies of the open Internet go, the Church of Scientology is pretty high on the list, and geeks had been raging against their attempted censorship of the Web for a few years at that point. For the geeks, the Internet promised a democratic vision of the future, where all ideas can compete on a level playing field, and no one's opinion can be snuffed out by a powerful interest group.

That utopian vision was challenged by the church, which wasn't used to people having the ability to expose its secrets on a mass scale. In 1991, Scott Goehring started alt.religion .scientology, a Usenet group dedicated to discussion of the Church, most of it critical. It became one of the most popular groups, and the church was not happy about it. On December 24, 1994, documents that could only have been gathered by an ex-member of the church showed up in the group. The church hired lawyers to issue cease and desist orders, citing copyright infringement, a tactic that is still used by organizations who've had their dirty deeds dragged into the light of day.

Then came the home raids, where federal marshals and church lawyers showed up at people's homes, confiscating servers and hard drives. The church took one critic to court in the United States, but after pressuring the remailer's owner to give up user logs, they were unable to prove that the defendant ever even used the remailer.

Conversely, courts ruled in favor of off-line anonymous pamphleteering in *McIntyre v. Ohio*. During that case, the court noted:

> Under our Constitution, anonymous pamphleteering is not a pernicious, fraudulent practice, but an honorable tradition of

advocacy and of dissent. Anonymity is a shield from the tyranny of the majority.

This case drew on the past two centuries of the courts upholding the right to pamphleteer anonymously, but it wouldn't be the last time the right was challenged within the context of the Internet. Some people feel that the Internet is something new, something different, and therefore requires new kinds of laws.

The following year, Georgia passed H.B. 1630, an amendment to the state's Computer Systems Protection Act, making it unlawful for any person or organization to knowingly transmit data through a computer network if such data contains a name or trademark used to falsely identify the sender. (Basically, you're not allowed to impersonate anyone else.) But the wording of the legislation was broad, and as a result, the amendment was challenged immediately, with a group of plaintiffs calling its constitutionality into question. The act prohibited the use of pseudonyms (in their words, a "false name") in order to protect against social ostracism, harassment, and discrimination. The court filed an injunction and the state of Georgia chose not to appeal. Although the law was meant to prevent one person from issuing a message under someone else's name without their consent, the language was vague and clearly written by someone who hadn't spent much time on the Internet, where most people speak with nicknames or handles.

The imposition of content-based speech restrictions, specifically on pseudonymity, were opposed by Georgia courts in *ACLU v. Miller* in 1997. The court ruled that the plaintiffs would succeed on their claim because these restrictions could potentially "chill" expressive activities. Again, the right to anonymous expression was preserved because statutory attacks on anonymity were clumsy, constitutionally vague, and overly broad.

Due to the historic protections for anonymous pamphleteering, those who wish to have the U.S. courts do away with online anonymity will have to prove that the Web is sui generis. Is an anonymous blog post effectively different than passing out pamphlets on a street corner? There are three common arguments: spectrum scarcity, pervasiveness, and lack of gatekeepers.

Spectrum scarcity is used as the basis for legislation in the realms of radio and television because the spectrum of frequencies used to broadcast signals were at one point finite. For instance, the dial on your FM radio can only pick up so many frequencies, so in this case, there's at least the veneer of legitimate justification for regulating the distribution of radio frequencies. Obviously this does not apply to the Web. The pervasiveness argument is often raised by "family values" politicians who argue that the Web is everywhere, messages can be used to reach millions instantaneously, and even children have access to it. So, according to them, censorship should apply, as it does in billboard marketing, for instance. This argument essentially boils down to, "Won't someone think of the children?" But the Web is different than a billboard. You can't stumble on a pornographic site in the same way you could accidentally view a pornographic highway billboard, assuming that sort of thing was legal—you would have to enter a search term to get there, or at least actively click on a link. The third argument rests on the idea that the Internet doesn't have any gatekeepers maintaining editorial control, the way a traditional publication would. But that's precisely why it's important to preserve freedom of speech on the Web and why censoring it is a lost cause. Sometimes gatekeepers wish to stifle minority opinion. Do we want a board of elites affirming all Web communication? These three arguments fall apart with cursory scrutiny.

Over the last two decades, politicians, law-enforcement officials, and special interest groups have petitioned the U.S. government to monitor activity on the Web, even suggesting that the Federal Communications Commission be given the same level of oversight on the Web that the organization enjoys within the realms of radio, television, wire, satellite, and cable. As of now, the FCC has little jurisdiction over the Web, with just four minimal "rules":

- Consumers are entitled to access the lawful Internet content of their choice.
- Consumers are entitled to run applications and use services of their choice, subject to the needs of law enforcement.
- Consumers are entitled to connect their choice of legal devices that do not harm the network.
- Consumers are entitled to competition among network providers, application and service providers, and content providers.

Still, the right to express oneself anonymously off-line has not been secured completely. In 2010 the Supreme Court decided against a group's right to sign a referendum without having their signatures vulnerable to public disclosure in *Doe v. Reed*. The state of Washington gives its citizens the right to challenge state laws by referendum if 4 percent of voters sign a petition to place a referendum on the ballot. The petition was required to include the names and addresses of the signers. However, the Washington Public Records Act states that private parties can obtain copies of government documents in order to allow citizens to ensure that the signatures are genuine. So the case partially rested on the determination of whether signing a petition was an act of public expression.

The group in question was made up of gay marriage opponents who had signed a referendum and, as a result, were being harassed. They claim they were "mooned," "flipped off," and "glared at," which apparently wasn't serious enough to convince judges to prevent the signatures from being revealed. Unlike the NAACP members in previous cases, these signers were not deemed to be in any actual danger. The judges ruled against the gay marriage opponents 8 to 1, with Clarence Thomas as the lone voice of dissent, arguing that the names should be revealed to several representatives, not the greater public.

But why, then, do we allow voters the anonymity of the polling booth, when voting for elected officials doesn't inspire widespread harassment? And who can decide what constitutes serious harm?

Although the general trend across human history has been toward open systems and freedom of speech, the sheer power of the Web has frightened us into balking at offering the same level of freedom for communication online that we allow it offline. This is not unreasonable: never before have individual evildoers had as much opportunity to cause social destruction. If you wanted to spread a message of hate before the Internet, the best you could do was print a run of pamphlets and hope that they got passed around whatever city you happened to be in. If you had the money, maybe you could hire people to spread the word in other cities. Mass media platforms like radio and TV are rife with gatekeepers and technological limitations that would prevent a rogue agent from disseminating volatile information. With the Web, one can spread a message to millions with the click of a button. The Internet will not offer editorial control.

Furthermore, the Internet is sui generis in that it allows for two-way conversations. If you print something I don't like on a platform that allows for comments, I can tell you about it. I can find out who your parents are and leave nasty messages on their office phones. I can determine where you live and slash your tires. I can hack into your e-mail account and ruin your credit. The Internet, unlike a pamphlet, doesn't just allow us to *say* things other people don't like. It allows us to *do* things. Sometimes bad things.

Today's anonymous activists have taken full advantage of that freedom, for better or for worse. We are just now seeing, a few years into the Web 2.0 era, the extent to which social networking amplifies a message, allowing activists to rally thousands of people around a cause in a matter of hours. So far, courts and legislators have mostly respected the rich tradition of anonymous free speech that has been pushing society forward, not just in the United States but across the globe, for centuries. It would be a dramatic break from historic trends if anonymous speech were to become an anathema in just a few decades.

In the next chapter, we meet a masked figure who seems to represent everything that those who would oppose anonymous speech fear—someone who might perhaps justify restrictions on namelessness. His name is Anonymous. Throughout the last year he has become a household name. He appears in one part of the world, strikes with glee, and disappears. He is a mystifying creature who seems to wriggle out of our grasp every time we attempt to pin him down. Anonymous grins widely at our fear and frustration, with rosy cheeks and a devilish wink. Enough idolization and fearmongering—it's time to take off the mask.

2

Anonymous Rises

*Your feelings mean nothing to us. . . . We have no culture, we
have no laws, written or otherwise. . . . We do not sleep, we do
not eat and we do not feel remorse. We will tear you apart from
outside and in, we have all the time in the world.*

—*Anonymous*

On September 17, 2011, I took a train from the top of Manhattan to the bottom, emerging from the hot subway to a light drizzle falling over the typically deserted (for the weekend) Financial District. I'd brought my tape recorder, hoping to capture some quotes from members of Anonymous, about whom I'd just written a book. Anonymous is an amorphous collective of hackers and pranksters who were born in the meme pool of an image board called 4chan, from where they launched attacks against individuals and groups for a laugh. Over the last several years, their aspirations have tended toward the political, and they now represent a growing antiauthority, anticensorship, antisurveillance sentiment.

When I started writing my last book, *Epic Win for Anonymous*, I set up a Google alert for the word "Anonymous," which would send an e-mail to my in-box every time a news outlet contained coverage of the group. I might get two or three news stories a day, and many of them had nothing to do with the collective about which I was writing—instead most of the stories dealt with anonymous corporate whistle-blowers or an upcoming film directed by Roland Emmerich called *Anonymous*.

During the summer following the completion of my book, that all changed. An Anonymous splinter group calling itself LulzSec had captivated the media with a series of sometimes harmless but always high-profile attacks. But it wasn't the attacks themselves that seemed to generate the most press attention; it was the swaggering Twitter feeds of LulzSec's members. Up until that point, Anonymous attacks were largely unexpected and isolated. It was difficult for the media to wrap a narrative around them. There was no hero, not even an anti-hero. This lack of a protagonist, or even an official spokesperson, makes it difficult for the media to explain what Anonymous is to an audience of people who expect criminal organizations to have some Al Capone–like mastermind. It also ramps up the risk of embarrassment, since anyone claiming to be Anonymous can say whatever he or she wants about the group's character and motives. If the press runs with it, and it turns out to be a troll, the reporters look infinitely foolish.

Everything changed when LulzSec members began to broadcast a daily salvo of tweets, which grew cockier as their list of victims expanded. The media finally found a foothold. These guys on Twitter, some of whom may not have had too much to do with actual hacking operations, gave the press their verifiable source. At least they could throw a caveat up on every story, saying, "We're not sure if this guy's the real deal, but he's the best we've got," and issue the occasional redaction if their source turned out to be a goof.

Within just a few months, I was getting several dozen Google alerts, sometimes over a hundred each day. Eventually even my Luddite parents had heard about the group, which only a few years earlier had been an obscure phenomenon limited to a handful of geeky Web communities, on the nightly news.

In the fall of 2011, Anonymous announced an unofficial partnership with several like-minded organizations, most notably *Adbusters* magazine, who'd launched a protest called Occupy Wall Street. The call to action was simple, as elucidated by one YouTube video:

> On September 17th, Anonymous will flood into Lower Manhattan, set up tents, kitchens, peaceful barricades, and occupy Wall Street for a few months. Once there, we shall incessantly repeat one simple demand in a plurality of voices: We want freedom. This is a nonviolent protest. We do not encourage violence in any way. The abuse and corruption of corporations, banks, and government ends here. Join us. We are anonymous. We are legion. We do not forgive. We do not forget. Wall Street, expect us.

When I visited Lower Manhattan that morning, I first came across well over a hundred policemen barricading off Wall Street's bronze bull. At a nearby square, I found the heart of the protest. Several hundred people gathered, passing around a megaphone to allow protestors to advocate a wide array of vaguely progressive talking points—everything from animal rights to immigration reform to an audit of the Federal Reserve. But to my surprise, I saw only a half dozen Guy Fawkes masks, the calling card of Anonymous. Clearly Anonymous's role in the protest was comparatively tiny. But as I walked through the crowds I noticed that a wide semicircle of cameras, microphones, and tired cameramen surrounded each person wearing a mask—while the mass of run-of-the-mill lefty protesters were ignored by the media.

But why?

Because the narrative of Anonymous as a mysterious band of elite cyber terrorists bringing down multinational corporations plays well on TV. They see themselves as modern-day Robin Hoods, and the press has reinforced this perception among the public. Even WikiLeaks founder Julian Assange has sported the mask while demonstrating outside of London's St. Paul's Cathedral. Anonymous's ability to generate press far outstrips their ability to hack and perform other cyber attacks. Their greatest strength is their knack for "hacking" the media, manipulating the pageview-hungry online media cycle by performing outrageous stunts, or even just merely threatening big attacks.

But this doesn't explain why the Anonymous story resonates so strongly with the average news viewer. The rise of Anonymous represents a strange new presence on the world stage. Unshackled by technology, Anonymous seems omnipresent, striking with precision, sometimes to make a political statement, sometimes just for fun. The government and corporate America have eyed them with a similar sort of fear masked by disdain and derision that the '60s counterculture received. Anonymous is something new, and it makes us uncomfortable. We can't pin it down, and just when we think we've figured them out, they morph into something else. Since that morning, rallies have sprung up across the globe in Rome, Madrid, San Francisco, London, and elsewhere. And a new story and catchphrase, "Occupy," grew in their stead.

The rise of Anonymous signifies a progression in activism brought about by technology, wherein leaders are not needed and egotists are despised (at least, that's how it works on paper). Members of Anon typically take great pains to avoid the emergence of recognizable figureheads, and, as a result, it has managed to stay alive. Members can wear the mask (real or figurative) today and take it off tomorrow, they can use it to protest economic disparities in New York or criminal drug cartels in Mexico.

Going deeper, the idea of anonymity as a broader social construct, especially online, also makes us uncomfortable. We fear cyberbullying and identity theft. We've spent the last two decades coming to terms with the idea that people can say nasty things about us on the Internet and there's nothing we can do about it. We shake our heads anxiously when we hear about a friend whose bank account was ripped off by someone who somehow got into her e-mail account and stole her password. We know the same thing could happen to us. We do our best to be safe online, but if these people can bring down the Central Intelligence Agency Web site, what can we possibly do to protect ourselves?

We are experiencing an evolution of human social behavior, but it remains to be seen if the Age of Anonymous will one day be recollected as an awkward technological adolescence or rather as the birth of the inevitable: the kind of world where people are free to try on new identities wherever they go. Anonymous is just one of the many manifestations of online anonymity, but it represents a global recognition of the value of anonymity and a growing unease with the erosion of personal identity ownership.

Anonymous can be whatever you want it to be, and the social power of your idea of "true Anonymous" lies in that idea's viral potential. In fact, the "idea" of Anonymous as a social activist group is just one particularly powerful iteration of this mysterious, ever-changing collective. Before 2007, they weren't in it to achieve social reform—they were in it for the lulz.

Life Ruiners

And now for a short history lesson. Anonymous was first conceived as a moniker for an ever-shifting group of people who engaged in hit-and-run cyber attacks against people on the Web who they generally felt "had it coming" for one reason or another. Their prime directive was to troll unsuspecting Internet personalities "for the lulz," or for fun. Trolling is a proactive form of schadenfreude, in which the goal is to upset the victim's emotional equilibrium through harassment, shock, deception, and general shenanigans. The term comes from the fishing lexicon, referring to dragging a baited hook or lure from a moving boat in order to entice gullible fish. Sometimes Anonymous's trolling is harmless, like when they gleefully manipulate the press into broadcasting phallic imagery (as in a notorious *Oprah* episode). Other times it tends toward the malicious. One favorite pastime deals with seeking out relatives of deceased teenagers and harassing them via social media.

Trolling on the Web was initially employed by forum members to inoculate new users (noobs) to the manners and mores of a Web community. It was a way of lightheartedly embarrassing noobs who'd behaved foolishly, that they might learn from their mistakes and become productive, in-the-know members of the group. It was also a way to defuse flaming—hostile communication on public forums. Clever trolls reminded impassioned users that it's best not to take things too seriously. It's just the Internet, after all.

In 1994, John Seabrook gave an account of his first experience with flaming in the *New Yorker*:

No one had ever said something like this to me before, and no one could have said this to me before: in any other medium, these words would be, literally, unspeakable. The guy couldn't have said this to me on the phone, because I would have hung up and not answered if the phone rang again, and he couldn't have said it to my face, because I wouldn't have let him finish. If this had happened to me in the street, I could have used my status as a physically large male to threaten the person, but in the on-line world my size didn't matter.

He goes on to describe how he contacted the Customer Service Department at CompuServe to ask if their customers were allowed to speak to each other this way. Of course, even then CompuServe had neither the resources nor the inclination to police the e-mail correspondence of its users.

My flame marked the end of my honeymoon with on-line communication. It made me see clearly that the lack of social barriers is also what is appalling about the net. The same anonymity that allows the twelve-year-old access to the professor allows a pedophile access to the twelve-year-old. The same lack of inhibitions that allows a woman to speak up in on-line meetings allows a man to ask the woman whether she's wearing any underwear. The same safe distance that allows you to unburden yourself of your true feelings allowed this guy to call me a toadying dipshit scumbag. A toadying dipshit scumbag!

Seabrook's breathless reaction to this random idiot's insults seems hilariously quaint to me, a guy who grew up with the Web and has always operated under the assumption that the Internet is full of faceless assholes and there's nothing you can do about it. In just a few years, our society has mostly come to terms with the rudeness of the Web, but Seabrook's reaction to his first flame is shared by many. We don't like trolls, but we deal with them. They continue to drive the discussion about anonymity on the Web.

There was a time when the Internet was only used by university professors, military researchers, and occasionally students, so the discourse was usually intelligent and congenial. Each passing year that changed, especially in September 1993, when a new batch of university students would gain access to Usenet. Old Usenetters often bemoan the "Eternal September" of '93, when America Online first gave its users free access to Usenet. Trolling was a fun way to pass down the community's in-jokes and standards of etiquette, especially when it seemed like they were in danger of being lost, overrun by noobs.

Which of course happened anyway. The social corners of the Internet became populated by people outside of traditionally geeky circles. Kids are on the Internet, and so are their moms tutt-tutting at the puerile discourse found there. And some network natives, when the wild and wooly nature of the Web became more slick and sterile, felt that they'd lost something special. But not everyone was willing to completely let go of the dangerous yet fun frontier-like character of the Web.

A decade after Seabrook's essay, a fifteen-year-old kid created a forum called 4chan that would gradually become the Internet's premier breeding ground for trolls. 4chan was initially conceived as an image board where geeks could discuss and share their favorite bits of Japanese pop culture, such as anime and manga. Given the Japanese pop cultural diaspora's predilection toward depictions of the extreme fringes of sexuality, 4chan quickly became a place where some of the most obscene, deviant content would flourish. 4chan, especially its "random" board called /b/, is a clearinghouse for stomach-turning imagery and links. Naturally, those with trollish inclinations found it a fitting home.

Adding to the attraction was 4chan's default anonymity and ephemerality, which encourage users to post content that they might not otherwise, were their names, or even a pseudonym, attached. Furthermore, it freed trolls with malevolent proclivities to harass fellow users, usually without consequence. It became a game to see how hard one could troll others, and members of Anonymous have gone to great lengths to outdo one another, resulting in trollish behaviors leaking outside the Web. Because 4chan's default name field was "anonymous," the community's users began referring to each other as "Anon." When 4chan trolls would reach out beyond their insular subculture, they began to call themselves "Anonymous," collectively.

Anonymous's first known trolls took place in the world of online gaming, where they would "grief" the often self-serious players with a variety of small annoyances. For instance, on Habbo Hotel, a global social networking site for teenagers, an early iteration of Anonymous called the Patriotic Nigras (a racially charged name designed to troll in itself) staged a mock suicide cult with the intent of freaking out their fellow players. In 2006, the Great Habbo Raid saw hundreds of Anons creating an identical avatar that they would use to block entrances, disrupt conversations, and flood chat rooms with racist and nonsensical content.

Anonymous also targeted furries in Second Life, a persistent virtual world that allows people to live out their (sometimes bestial) fantasies online. Second Life is home to many kinds of people, but it has a noticeably large population of furries, people who role-play as fuzzy critters. Early Anons, under the Patriotic Nigras name, created a town within Second Life populated by the mutilated corpses of furry avatars. Furries and other young gamers were perceived by Anons as low-hanging fruit due to their passion for the game world. Their cries of indignation and complaints to moderators delighted the trolls and only encouraged further harassment. Journalist Julian Dibbell has studied online trolls for the last decade. In an interview for *Wired*, he captured a quote from one mischievous EVE Online player that crystallizes the modus operandi of the modern troll: "The way that you win in EVE is you basically make life so miserable for someone else that they actually quit the game and don't come back."

By 2006, Anons realized that they not only had the ability to wreak significant havoc on the Web, but off-line as well. They became infamous for "raiding" the memorial Web sites for deceased teenagers. They broke out into the real world, or "IRL" for In Real Life, by calling the parents of the recently deceased, pretending to be the ghosts of their dead children. They terrorized radio shows and cable access programs with prank calls, using 4chan's boards to mobilize the troops for their raids. A few called in bomb threats and were subsequently arrested.

There are documents frequently passed around on 4chan that educate trolls with the latest in harassment methods. These pages draw from the Web's rich heritage of antisocial literature such as *The Anarchist Cookbook*. 4chan trolls typically use the Web as a way to harass their victims. The "Ruin Life Tactics" doc details some of the most common Web-based pranks. These run from ordering prank deliveries to posting the victim's address on Craigslist with a request for volunteers to indulge their rape fantasy.

Other attacks are dead simple:

> Report the guy to the police as an anonymous tip for suspicion of selling drugs. Result:
> Police harassment
> ???
> Epic win

"Let's ruin her life," someone will say. Usually these calls to action are ignored, but every so often trolling efforts picked up steam.

Such was the case with Parry Aftab, a self-described Internet safety expert and lawyer who is routinely trotted out on *Good Morning America* and similar morning shows every time a case of cyberbullying catches the attention of TV producers. In July 2011, her home was swarmed by a SWAT team responding to a call they thought had come from inside her home. The caller told the police he was armed and had two hostages inside Aftab's home. When the police arrived, they shot tear gas inside Aftab's windows, only to find her cat. The prankster had used VoIP technology to mask his identity and remains unknown. This prank is known among Anonymous as "SWAT-ing."

I found myself on the receiving end of some low-level trolling when Anonymous found out that I'd published a book about their exploits. Even though I painted a rather kind portrayal of the group, they still don't like it when people talk about them. The first of two so-called Rules of the Internet dictate that (1) Don't talk about /b/, and (2) Don't talk about /b/. Simply by explaining their culture to a mainstream audience, I had broken these cherished rules and taken part in an ongoing process of demystifying 4chan and Anonymous.

They sent me thirty pizzas in one night, including one $90 pie, with extra of every available topping. I've been flooded with junk mail, spam, and unwanted magazine subscriptions. Many of my relatives were targeted on Facebook. Most hilariously, my middle-aged aunt received a rather saucy message from one "Cole Stryker" asking her to meet me for an illicit midnight rendezvous. Vague death threats trickled in.

For the most part I was unfazed by Anonymous's harassment. I'd been studying their culture for years, so I knew what to expect. Extreme trolls like this rely heavily on the fear and ignorance of their victims. It's not very fun to antagonize someone who's already aware of the usual tricks, has prepared his friends and family in advance, and has taken measures to shore up his data security. Despite my foresight, it's still unsettling that a faceless psychopath from across the globe was able to obtain my home address within minutes of discovering the existence of my book project.

"For Great Justice!"

Some Anons, however, attempted to use their collective power for good, applying their unique brand of vigilante justice to actual evildoers. They've used their collaborative sleuthing to unearth several animal abusers and are known to hand over the information of child pornographers to authorities. *Dateline NBC*'s *To Catch a Predator* segment features tech-savvy detectives luring pedophiles into a police trap by posing as children online. Anonymous uses the same tactics to ascertain the personal information of pedophiles and then forwards the information to police. Their efforts have led to several arrests.

Most recently, Anonymous has launched Operation Darknet, a campaign against child porn. On October 14, 2011, Anonymous became aware of a massive child porn cache made up of over forty Web sites, most notably Lolita City. These sites operated through Tor "onion routing" software, which allows people to communicate and share files incognito. Anonymous claims to have brought down 100GB of child porn and publicly leaked 1,569 user account details. But that wasn't enough. Anonymous wanted IP addresses. Your IP (Internet Protocol) address is like your computer's address on the Internet. Every

Internet connection has its own IP address. If Anon could get its hands on IP addresses, they could pinpoint the geographic locations of their targets.

Tired of waiting around for the police to act on their leak, a few enterprising Anons created a "honeypot," a disguised trap on a computer network that can be monitored and used to collect data about users interacting with information on or passing through the honeypot. They are used by researchers, law enforcement, and spammers to achieve different goals, some nobler than others.

In this case, the honeypot was disguised as an update to Tor, the anonymizing network favored by child pornographers because it allows them to share illicit materials. Security software developers release updates periodically because they have to stay one step ahead of hackers who are constantly figuring out ways to bypass security systems. Those seeking child porn are therefore highly incentivized to download the latest Tor updates so as to ensure the maximum amount of privacy available.

So when an update was announced that Tor would be receiving a software update, nearly two hundred people jumped at the opportunity to download it, not stopping to think about where the update was coming from. In fact, the update was the product of a twenty-four-hour Anonymous coding marathon. Anons caught wind of a legitimate Tor update that was on the way by hanging out in a chat room used by Tor developers.

Typically, Tor users' traffic is routed through a series of nodes, making it virtually impossible to trace the source of the traffic. But Anonymous's trap sent users through a honeypot node, which enabled them to log the IP addresses of 190 users, which were then leaked publicly and used to dig up social media profiles, and in some cases, actual names.

Thus we are able to see Anonymous's first tastes of righteous indignation and the euphoric rush that goes along with achieving victory over perceived evildoers. At some point the collective realized that it had the power to make lasting social change, something they could be proud of, as opposed to random mean pranks. We come to find that Anonymous's heritage can be divided, if not neatly, into three broad eras, which are better represented thematically than chronologically, since the defining properties of each era bleed into the others.

The first age of Anonymous was marked by indiscriminate and often malicious attacks against innocent bystanders, such as eleven-year old YouTube divas and goofy radio hosts. The second, by seemingly random acts of Internet vigilantism aimed at individual animal abusers and pedophiles. The third era, when Anon went political and transcended the boundaries of the Web, is the subject of the next chapter.

3

Anonymous Goes Political

A building is a symbol, as is the act of destroying it. Symbols are given power by people. A symbol, in and of itself, is powerless, but with enough people behind it, blowing up a building can change the world. —V, V for Vendetta

ON JANUARY 21, 2008, a video appeared on YouTube featuring a digitized voice that described a vague, mysterious group of vigilantes who would bring a reckoning to the Church of Scientology.

Hello, leaders of Scientology. We are Anonymous.

Over the years, we have been watching you. Your campaigns of misinformation; your suppression of dissent; your litigious nature, all of these things have caught our eye. With the leakage of your latest propaganda video into mainstream circulation, the extent of your malign influence over those who have come to trust you as leaders has been made clear to us. Anonymous has therefore decided that your organization should be destroyed. For the good of your followers, for the good of mankind—and for our own enjoyment—we shall proceed to expel you from the Internet and systematically dismantle the Church of Scientology in its present form. We recognize you as a serious opponent, and we are prepared for a long, long campaign. You will not prevail forever against the angry masses of the body politic. Your methods, hypocrisy, and the artlessness of your organization have sounded its death knell.

You have nowhere to hide because we are everywhere. We cannot die; we are forever. We're getting bigger every day—and solely by the force of our ideas, malicious and hostile as they often are. If you want another name for your opponent, then call us Legion, for we are many.

Knowledge is free. We are Anonymous. We are Legion. We do not forgive. We do not forget. Expect us.

The video was an overnight global sensation and its viral success helped solidify Anonymous's new role as a pseudopolitical activist group. The dark, mysterious vibe of the video further defined the group's aesthetic, as did the dramatic verbiage. From that point forward, nearly every video coming out of Anonymous would close with the advertising tagline-like words, "We are Anonymous. We are Legion. We do not forgive. We do not forget. Expect us." They sounded like superheroes . . . or maybe supervillains. It was as if the freedom-fighting vigilante V from Alan Moore's comic had stepped into the real world. Millions of viewers waited to see what would come next.

Trolling for a Good Cause: Project Chanology

Of course, anti-Scientology sentiment is nothing new on the Internet. The broader movement can be traced back to the Usenet era. The Church of Scientology has been known to file vicious lawsuits against those who would speak out against their practices. This method of censorship lies in direct opposition to the ideals of many of the Internet's most influential early voices. Many folks were drawn to early bulletin board systems in the '80s because they offered an open environment to discuss ideas freely on a level playing field. It didn't matter how much clout you had in the real world. On the Internet, if you had something interesting to say, someone would listen. Many shared the principle of freedom of information in those days, and the sentiment has trickled down throughout the years, continuing to thrive in geeky circles.

Remember alt.religion.scientology? It was populated by free-speech enthusiasts and ex-church members who'd decided to speak out against perceived injustices. The Church of Scientology was notorious for suppressing critical information about the religion in the press, so the Web offered a safe place for critics to spread awareness. The subsequent home raids were seen as a grave injustice that motivated them to spread the word throughout the Web. Anti-Scientology sentiment continued to spread throughout the '90s and '00s, with the church and anti-Scientologists engaging in small skirmishes here and there. It wasn't until Anonymous got involved with Project Chanology in 2008 that the anti-Scientology movement would explode onto the front pages of the mainstream media.

The floodgates opened with a leak of a bizarre internal video starring actor and prominent Scientologist Tom Cruise, who is shown in the video describing strange spiritual phenomena over the *Mission Impossible* theme music. When Gawker founder Nick Denton posted the footage on January 15, 2008, he called Cruise a "complete fanatic," declaring, "If Tom Cruise jumping on Oprah's couch was an 8 on the scale of scary, this is a 10."

Of course, the church tried to suppress the video, but they were operating in a different world than the one they had known in the early '90s. Having information taken down from the Web once it's posted is now impossible. The video was successfully removed several times, only for it to pop up elsewhere.

The clip went viral within minutes, and one member of Anonymous saw an opportunity to strike. Gregg Housh, whose affiliation with Anonymous has since been made public, claims to have posted the aforementioned "Message to Scientology," just a few days after the Tom Cruise video leak. Much to his surprise, his call to action received millions of views and reignited a global anti-Scientology movement, this time under the veil of anonymity. After all, the church can't litigate what it can't see.

Anonymous was more malicious in their attacks against the church than previous critics, employing a new technology this time around, something that helped to collectivize their mayhem: the Low Orbit Ion Cannon. The LOIC is a piece of software named after a fictional sci-fi weapon that allows dozens, hundreds, or thousands of people to point their computers at a single Web site, overloading the site's server until it's taken off-line. If a site is operated by a smart system administrator, precautions can be taken in advance because he or she will see it coming and prepare accordingly. But smaller sites with fewer resources are sometimes rendered helpless. Well-written firewalls can filter out the junk traffic, but right now there are a lot of companies vulnerable to a DDoS (distributed denial-of-service) attack initiated through LOIC. It's not anonymous by default, but many LOIC users can route their traffic through Tor. Even then, it's risky, and several Anon arrests have resulted from these low-level attacks since the Scientology protest.

LOIC was important in the evolution of Anonymous as a hacktivist group because it granted users instant hacking ability, though most real hackers would scoff at calling LOIC hacking, since it doesn't involve any actual network infiltration—just download the software, set a target, and fire away. Even if it wasn't technically hacking, it could still cause damage, and this surely provided Anons with at least the intoxicating perception of power.

Anons also sent bogus faxes and prank calls. But more important, they organized real-world protests outside church property. This was a completely new development in Anon tactics. Hundreds of people around the world would show up at Scientology buildings and picket for hours. Some wore Guy Fawkes masks, some didn't. Some dressed up as Darth Vader or various Internet memes. For the most part it was lighthearted fun. They held hilarious signs referencing Internet ephemera and, in some cases, probably generated more confusion than awareness of the church's evils. The group's freewheeling anarchy coupled with its mystery enchanted the media, and soon Anonymous's Guy Fawkes mask became the symbol of a genuine new global activist movement.

The most important outcome of Project Chanology was the church's defanging. Anonymous attacked Scientology on so many fronts that it was virtually impossible for them to file suit against every critic, even the ones who openly divulged their identities. A DDoS bit IRL (In Real Life). Today, people are mostly free to say whatever they wish about the group with no consequences. This was a significant victory for free speech. The Church of Scientology has historically been one of the most litigious organizations in terms of suppressing information on the Web. Anonymous, through sheer numbers, overloaded the church's system for dealing with information leaks and critical speech. You might even say that they hacked it. Say what you will about Anonymous's nastier endeavors, this was a significant, if unheralded, victory for freedom of speech.

Throughout the next few years, Anonymous continued to fire potshots at the establishment here and there, leaking the contents of vice presidential hopeful Sarah Palin's e-mail account, antagonizing the Tea Party, the Iranian government, the Motion Picture Association of America, the Recording Industry Association of America, KISS's Gene Simmons, and an assortment of self-promoting Internet microcelebrities.

With the rise of the social Web, Anon recognized that their stomping grounds were becoming increasingly commoditized, and thus tame. Their mischief was a way to preserve the strangeness and unpredictability of the Web. After all, many geeks turned to the Internet because it gave them a place to have fun and be in control in a way that they couldn't IRL.

The massive press attention that Anonymous received for Project Chanology in 2007 was nothing compared to the scrutiny they would receive, when a series of high-profile hacks and a seemingly endless stream of tweets, YouTube videos, and blog posts would enable the media to easily and quickly perpetuate Anon's message. Anonymous dominated mainstream media headlines on a near-daily basis in 2011.

A sea change had taken place within the ranks of Anonymous. The group was becoming less about random acts of mischief and more about a concerted activist effort using technology to harass those who would attempt to stifle, censor, or manipulate the free flow of information. Veteran hackers can say what they will about the actual skills of the average Anon, but they can't deny that the group has figured out how to take control of various systems and manipulate them to their own ends. This should solidify their place in hacker history.

To this day, the mainstream media misinterprets the nature of Anonymous. They have no leader, no official spokesperson, no manifesto, or even any guiding principle apart from an intent to disrupt. This impulse manifests itself in wildly varying ways, from bullying tweens to exposing high-level bankers. To prevent confusion, I refer to Anonymous in this book as a group. In truth, it would be more accurate to describe Anonymous as a brand—a vague brand of civil disobedience that means different things to different people. When a message appears on Twitter claiming that Anonymous is going to "kill Facebook" on November 5th reporters asked, "Is this an official stance?" Asking that question belies a fundamental misunderstanding of how the Anonymous brand works. Anonymous efforts are never "official" in the sense that they're approved by a governing board or a vote. Anonymous's endeavors live and die by their memetic, or viral, potential.

Does attacking a particular target resonate with enough people? Is it something that will inspire them to share the news with their friends? If so, that's as close to "official" as an Anonymous operation is going to get. Anonymous is a "memeocracy," in that their goals and targets are determined not by a governing organization, as in most groups, but organically, each living or dying depending on their chances of going viral—a difficult thing to engineer. In many cases, operations have become "official" because they play well in the mainstream media, which helps to get the word out to far-flung

Anons who might not be as active in Anon communication channels. When CNN runs a story about a potential Anonymous campaign, asking, "Is X a Genuine Anonymous Effort?" in the headline, they've answered their own question. It's often a self-fulfilling prophecy.

In December 2010, Anonymous had thrown its support behind the leak distribution group WikiLeaks. When it was announced that MasterCard, Visa, and PayPal refused to process donations to the group after the organization released a massive cache of classified U.S. diplomatic cables, Anonymous perceived this as a blatant example of government collusion with financial institutions. Within two days they pulled off a series of DDoS attacks against the companies' Web sites. The form of the attacks was nothing new, but the importance of the targets was. Inconveniencing the Church of Scientology was one thing, but if a bunch of loosely organized computer geeks could bring down massive multinational corporations, who could be safe? The coming year would be marked by a public unease, perhaps not entirely unfounded, that the world's security systems could not keep up with the ingenuity and agility of Anonymous. This fear manifested itself even in the security industry, and security firms as well as the Department of Homeland Security began to scrutinize the collective's activity. Dozens of home raids followed, marked by the Federal Bureau of Investigation seizing hard drives across the United States. By this time, Anonymous had captured the imagination of the mainstream media and were portrayed as everything from a radical leftist group of cyberterrorists to an anarchic band of sociopathic computer geniuses.

In January 2011, Anonymous ramped up their political activism, bringing down government Web sites in Tunisia and Egypt on account of their censorship of WikiLeaks and to assist activists with spreading information, creating guides for dissenters to spread word of their protests anonymously on the Web.

Anonymous Humiliates HBGary Federal

The following month, Aaron Barr, the chief executive of the security firm HBGary Federal, declared that he'd infiltrated Anonymous and would unmask the collective at an upcoming conference. Then the *Financial Times* published a piece asserting as much. The media was hungry to put a face to Anonymous, and Aaron Barr was understandably thrilled to claim such a discovery, which put him at the forefront of media frenzy. He believed that he could determine the real names of Anonymous's leaders using log-in information from the entirely public Anonops IRC (Internet relay chat) chat room, where a lot of chatter among low-level Anons took place. Barr and his associates were poised to bask in the glory of unmasking one of the security industry's hottest villains du jour.

That afternoon a message appeared on the front page of HBGary's Web site reading, "This domain has been seized by Anonymous under section #14 of the rules of the Internet."[1] The message was accompanied by a link to a file containing tens of thousands of e-mails that had been taken from HBGary's servers. To add insult to injury, the information Barr

---

[1] According to a jokey list of rules for the Internet that is often passed around 4chan: "Do not argue with trolls, it means they win."

gathered came to nothing. It was inaccurate in places and use-less to others.

The leaked e-mails revealed a truly incredible story of in-trigue. HBGary Federal, along with Berico Technologies and Palantir Technologies—two tech contractors who also worked regularly with government clients—and law firm Hunton & Williams joined forces to serve high-profile clients such as Bank of America and the U.S. Chamber of Commerce under the name Team Themis.

Julian Assange of WikiLeaks claimed that his organization possessed proof of corruption at Bank of America. So BoA went to Team Themis to come up with a plan to discredit Assange. Team Themis proposed DDoS attacks and a smear campaign against journalists who supported WikiLeaks, such as Salon.com's Glenn Greenwald. Another e-mail read:

> I think we need to highlight people like Glenn Greenwald. . . .
> It is this level of support we need to attack. These are established
> professionals that have a liberal bent, but ultimately most of
> them if pushed will choose professional preservation over cause,
> such is the mentality of most business professionals. Without the
> support of people like Glenn WikiLeaks would fold.

HBGary also proposed the release of fake information to WikiLeaks so that their accurate accusations would be muddled with planted untruths, and therefore easily discredited. Fur-thermore, Barr was personally scraping data from potential clients' social networking profiles as well as those of their rela-tives in an attempt to frighten clients into appreciating his abil-ity to dig up information.

> A bit of what I have on [redacted]. He was hard to find on
> Facebook as he has taken some precautions to be found. He
> isn't even linked with his wife but I found him. I also have a list

of his friends and have defined an angle if I was to target him. He has attachment to UVA, a member of multiple associations dealing with IP, e-discovery, and nearly all of his facebook friends are of people from high school. So I would hit him from one of these three angles. I am tempted to create a person from his high school and send him a request, but that might be over-stepping it.

Anonymous found the news supremely ironic, considering that they often used the same rudimentary tactics to uncover information about their targets. In fact, they were granted access to HBGary's server when Anons used similar techniques to impersonate HBGary CEO Greg Hoglund.

HBGary Federal was also developing complex persona man-agement software, which essentially would allow clients, in this case the U.S. Air Force, to conjure thousands of fake social net-working profiles, or "sock puppets," to artificially spread gov-ernment propaganda through a process called "astroturfing," a faked version of a grassroots movement.

Perhaps most disconcertingly, all the confirmed conspiracies of media manipulation and social engineering that were pres-ent in the leaked e-mails imply that the corruption was not lim-ited to HBGary Federal or even its clients. After all, if a random leak like this inspired by a few prankish geeks was able to turn up such damning information, what are all the hundreds of other defense and intelligence contractors hiding? Are we really as free as we think we are? Is the entire security industry rotten to the core? Is the U.S. government engaged in wide-spread "gray ops," manipulating mass and social media with sock puppetry and falsehoods?

The fallout from the e-mail leak was devastating for HBGary and Barr. Their partners immediately distanced themselves from the company and many involved in suspicious e-mail correspondence issued statements declaring they were unaware of Barr's questionable behavior.

Anon's absolute humiliation of Aaron Barr and HBGary put them in the papers to an unprecedented degree. Between this victory and their attacks on MasterCard, Visa, and PayPal, Anonymous had arrived. At this point they could be seen as the reckless little brother of the more responsible WikiLeaks, who generally attempted to work inside the law.

Many Anons had turned to the Internet as a last bastion of free speech and privacy, but the findings at HBGary and elsewhere revealed that the Web was in danger of becoming yet another tool of the establishment, closely monitored and manipulated, which would seem to fly in the face of the idea of the Internet as an open forum for all beliefs and opinions. Throughout the next five months, Anonymous continued investigating the intelligence industry through OpMetalGear. Powerful defense contractors such as Unveillance, ManTech, and Booz Allen Hamilton came under fire with DDoSs and the theft of sensitive documents.

Throughout the next few months, Anonymous expanded due to all the press attention, and they began to branch out, hoping to continue the momentum built from the attack on HBGary. OpSony began when Sony sued a man for "jailbreaking" (bypassing the limitations on a piece of hardware placed by manufacturers in order to make a gadget do what it's not supposed to do) his PlayStation 3 console. Anonymous, being made up largely of computer geeks who admire and collaborate on jailbreaking, took umbrage. On April 17, 37,500 Sony customer accounts were compromised by an unknown entity. Some Anons claimed responsibility; others insisted Anonymous had nothing to do with the attack. The attack cost Sony millions.

In May an Anonymous splinter group called LulzSec, later revealed to be made up of several of the people behind the HBGary attacks, attacked Fox.com because they'd called rapper Common, who'd been selected to perform at the White House, "vile." They leaked the social network profiles and names of seventy-three thousand *X Factor* (a Fox show) contestants. They hacked into a PBS Web site, retaliating for a documentary series that they felt portrayed Julian Assange in a negative light. They defaced the home page and posted a jokey story about deceased rapper Tupac Shakur living in New Zealand. Throughout June 2011 they attacked dozens of Web sites in a seemingly indiscriminate rampage of lighthearted mischief.

But there was a serious element to this era as well. Operation Anti-Security began around this time, declared by LulzSec and Anonymous to be in protest of government censorship and surveillance of the Internet, along with several secondary issues like the war on drugs and racial profiling. They felt it was time to take back the Web from those who would corrupt it with censorship.

Salutations Lulz Lizards,

As we're aware, the government and white-hat security terrorists across the world continue to dominate and control our Internet ocean. Sitting pretty on cargo bays full of corrupt booty, they think it's acceptable to condition and enslave all vessels in sight. Our Lulz Lizard battle fleet is now declaring immediate and unremitting war on the freedom-snatching moderators of 2011.

Welcome to Operation Anti-Security (#AntiSec)—we encourage any vessel, large or small, to open fire on any government or agency that crosses their path. We fully endorse the flaunting of the word "AntiSec" on any government Web site defacement or physical graffiti art. We encourage you to spread the word of AntiSec far and wide, for it will be remembered. To increase efforts, we are now teaming up with the Anonymous collective and all affiliated battleships.

Whether you're sailing with us or against us, whether you hold past grudges or a burning desire to sink our lone ship, we invite you to join the rebellion. Together we can defend ourselves so that our privacy is not overrun by profiteering gluttons. Your hat can be white, gray or black, your skin and race are not important. If you're aware of the corruption, expose it now, in the name of Anti-Security.

Top priority is to steal and leak any classified government information, including email spools and documentation. Prime targets are banks and other high-ranking establishments. If they try to censor our progress, we will obliterate the censor with cannon fire anointed with lizard blood.

It's now or never. Come aboard, we're expecting you . . .

History begins today.

What followed was a dizzying series of global hacks, leaks, and other attacks targeting government contractors, banks, intelligence agencies, media outlets, and more. The mainstream media followed Anonymous's every move that summer. As a result, the group experienced splintering, infighting, and attacks from outside hackers like never before.

Inevitably law enforcement was able to catch up with Anonymous and started making arrests. By the end of the summer, Anonymous's attacks seemed to come to a close. The gloating tweets and other missives continued, however, insisting that Anon would continue fighting the good fight.

Fighting Fat Cats and
Drug Lords

Meanwhile, a resurgence of Anonymous protests began IRL. In August, Anonymous protested in San Francisco when Bay Area Rapid Transit shut down cell phone service in the subway stations to discourage protests that were already taking place in response to a police shooting.

On the other side of the country, Anonymous played a key role in kick-starting one of the most widespread protest movements since the Vietnam War. It began with journalist David DeGraw's 2010 book, *The Economic Elite vs. The People of the United States of America*, which declared, "The harsh truth is that 99% of the U.S. population no longer has political representation." DeGraw formed the 99 Percent Movement, a social network for people who wished to discuss economic and legal reforms. When the site was attacked by unknown hackers, Anonymous stepped in to help DeGraw set up a more secure site. This collaboration grew into increased sympathy among Anons for the so-called 99 Percent. Anon launched Operation Empire State Rebellion, with the goal of ousting Federal Reserve chairman Ben Bernanke, complete with a planned physical protest in Zuccotti Park, near Wall Street in downtown Manhattan. But the event was a flop, with little turnout.

Meanwhile, *Adbusters*, which had no relationship with Anonymous, was developing their own protest, Occupy Wall Street, which was set to go down September 17. Although Anonymous never worked with *Adbusters* in any official capacity, they helped get the word out, spreading the message throughout social networks and chat rooms along with creating posters, videos, and other iconography to help crystallize the protest as a legitimate movement.

When I visited Zuccotti Park on September 17, there were only a few hundred people there, but those numbers quickly grew thanks to an overwhelming amount of media exposure, largely driven by America's fascination with the shadowy group called Anonymous. When a police officer was caught pepper-spraying a group of nonthreatening women, Anonymous dug up his personal information and released it to the Web, along with that of several other policemen and prominent bankers. Around this time, some Anons claimed that they were going to "erase the NYSE from the Internet." Another said that Anon's next project would be to "kill Facebook."

Anyone who'd been following Anonymous for longer than a few weeks would know better than to report these as official communiqués. Even within the weird universe of Anonymous attacks, they were particularly over-the-top, vague, and quixotic. But that didn't stop every mainstream media outlet from reporting them. Sure enough, within forty-eight hours most had issued follow-up pieces, clarifying that the calls to action might be coming from a "rogue" group of Anons or might be hoaxes entirely. The problem with this kind of coverage is that it assumes there is such a thing as an official stance from Anonymous.

Anonymous's relationship with the media reveals a serious flaw with modern reportage. Journalists are so tremendously incentivized by pageviews that they are eager to jump on a story before anyone else gets to it. This is nothing new. What has changed in the last few decades is that a site can sometimes "own" a particular keyword in search engine results pages if they're able to write about it first, racking up massive amounts of views in the long run. So "report first, ask questions later" journalism has made it difficult for nuanced, reasoned under-standings of Anonymous to push through into the mainstream.

Meanwhile, a few Anons were fighting corruption on a dif-ferent front. On October 6, a YouTube video was released chal-lenging Los Zetas, a multibillion-dollar Mexican drug cartel. The video, part of Operation Cartel, accused the Zetas of kid-napping, theft, blackmail, and preying on the hardworking cit-izens of Veracruz, Mexico. Furthermore, it lashed out against the gang's "most loyal servants," the police, and other authority figures who either actively collaborate with the Zetas or look the other way when confronted with corruption. The video threatened to expose these collaborators by publishing their photos and contact information, ending with the usual "We do not forgive. We do not forget."

Paperstorm was a global pamphleteering operation con-ducted by Anons, with the goal of spreading information about the cartel on the streets. One of their members was allegedly kidnapped by the cartel, and Anonymous threatened to leak sensitive information implicating specific cartel members. In response, one "Anon" named Barrett Brown, who had served as a self-appointed public face for Anonymous as a whole, an-nounced that Anonymous possessed twenty-five thousand stolen government e-mails that would be used to expose secret cartel collaborators. Other Anons seemed to balk due to the danger of the operation, but Brown claimed that he and several cohorts would move forward with the leak. On November 4, the day before the reveal was scheduled to take place, Brown claimed that the Zetas had capitulated, releasing their kid-napped comrade:

> The Anon who had been kidnapped last month by the Zetas has been released, although it appears that the Zetas concerned did not know that the individual was the Anon whose release had

been demanded by those who instigated #OpCartel. As such, no bargain has been fulfilled. Meanwhile, those who have been in possession of the e-mails have promised to provide them to me alone, which is to say that everything that proceeds from now on is my own work, and not that of Anonymous. Any reprisals against anyone other than myself, then, will have no effect.

Brown told several journalists that he would be assisting several parties to assess the contents of the e-mails, particularly portions dealing with Zetas collaborators. He lashed out at journalists who would dare to call his motives into question, labeling those who would suggest that he back off in the face of the bloodiest drug cartel in Mexico's history "degenerate."

The idea that I should refrain from assisting in the naming of probable criminals operating in a foreign country without a working judicial system lest I be murdered is a cowardly sentiment. No individual living in the free world should refrain from working to fight injustice simply because there is a possibility of retaliation.

He went on to lambast a "sick culture that is destined for destruction and replacement," referring to a cowardly America who does not deserve the freedom it enjoys, since it is so clearly unwilling to assist the persecuted journalists in Mexico.

If, by some chance, I am indeed killed by the Zetas, I will at least not have to contend ever again with the irritating and, frankly, faggy outpourings of a population that has proven itself incompetent to rule the empire that has been provided to it on the backs of others. Amrite?

No police report was ever filed for the alleged kidnapping. No prominent journalists have officially confirmed the contents of Brown's cache of e-mails, and everything that's been reported about this story has been based on Brown's own testimony. It's also worth noting that Brown recently signed a book deal with Amazon that, according to him, is "well into six figures."

Whether or not Barrett Brown is using Operation Cartel to increase his status, the frenzy of mainstream media coverage surrounding Operation Cartel speaks to the nature of coverage of Anonymous in general. The story is full of intrigue—the cartel has been known to leave critical bloggers hanging headless from highway overpasses, but as of this writing, there's really nothing concrete about Brown's narrative. He claims to be holding evidence close to his chest in order to protect the livelihood of innocents who might be related to the kidnapping. Regardless of the authenticity of his claims, Brown has proven that nearly anyone can claim to speak on behalf of Anonymous and receive scads of unquestioning media gratification.

In the first few months of 2012 we've seen Anonymous operations popping up every few days, all over the world, with wildly varying goals. Anons have teamed up with the People's Liberation Front in Nigeria, promising hacks against the government in retaliation to the removal of a fuel subsidy that resulted in a drastic decrease in quality of life among the majority of Nigerians. In Poland, Slovenia, France, Greece, Austria, and elsewhere, Anonymous initiated a series of DDoS attacks against government Web sites in protest of the country's signing of the Anti-Counterfeiting Trade Agreement, or ACTA. They have lashed out at various U.S. government agencies for shutting down Megaupload. They have gone after neo-Nazi groups in Germany.

This political branch of Anonymous is the latest manifestation of nameless activism, surely the most theatrical we've ever seen, informed by the strange culture of 4chan, which itself takes cues from Hollywood action flicks featuring masked heroes spouting pithy one-liners. The reaction to Anonymous among old-time activists has been mixed. Some embrace this freewheeling form of social disruption; others find it to be a repulsive and childish movement that actually does harm to the broader progression of freedoms. They've broken into Syrian government officials' networks, brought down the American Israel Public Affairs Committee (AIPAC) Web site. They've declared war on foes as powerful as organized religion and Interpol.

The Anonymous banner of hacktivism and street protest has grown increasingly customizable, to the point where any anti-authoritarian cause can be subsumed into the brand. Anonymous activists in Spain have almost nothing in common with those in Syria, and yet both groups are utilizing the same Guy Fawkes imagery and revolutionary rhetoric. The memetic property of Anonymous represents a new way for traditionally marginalized groups (at least, those who see themselves as such) to strike back against entrenched global powers. In the pre-Anonymous era, protest groups would do everything they could to increase their visibility in order to generate awareness about a social injustice. Governments are able to use the Web as a tool for censorship and suppression of dissenting voices, so these traditional tactics have become a liability. Now hacktivists use technology to turn the tables. Anonymous has flipped the paradigm, demonstrating the value of integrating one's local political concerns, weaving them into the thicker, stronger fabric of a broader, more eminently viral protest movement.

Furthermore, Anonymous's decentralized, horizontal structure prevents the rise of a leader. I don't believe Anonymous will ever see a Martin Luther King Jr.–like figurehead. Not only do they not need one, they don't want one. This structure represents more purely the populist ethos behind the protest than any other protest movement in human history. It's one-size-fits-all activism, and its amorphousness and agility will work for you whether you're protesting tyranny in Tunisia or drug cartels in Mexico. The rise of Anonymous, despite its wildly varying aims, illustrates a crucial shift in the way ordinary people speak truth to power, not by shouting more loudly on the ground, but by synthesizing their local protest with the vaguely antiestablishment goals of this global protest "brand." Regardless of what you might think about the ethical questions whirling around Anonymous, this is a notable accomplishment.

In terms of the identity wars, Anonymous's place isn't easy to determine. On the one hand, they represent a tremendously powerful tool to instantly mobilize thousands of like-minded protestors in the streets and through the wires. They are adept at building awareness around a specific issue. They are agile because there is no administrative inertia. Someone says, "We doin' this?" and then it happens, or it doesn't.

But at the same time, they are a volatile bunch. Without an official leader, it's difficult to determine what the group actually wants. It's not outside the realm of possibility that Anonymous will be pulled apart in the coming months. Its brand might not be able to withstand the dilution of a hundred different causes. Perhaps most important, Anonymous isn't going to be as sexy in 2013 as it was the year before. They're all over the airwaves, like your favorite indie rock band that just got signed to a major label. Anonymous might still be difficult to analyze, but their captivating inscrutability may have faded. A lot of the people who were into Anonymous a year ago have likely moved on. For some, the thrill is gone, and now it's just a bunch of noobs: self-righteous ones, without the skills to back it up.

Anonymous represents an evolution as much as a revolution. In the past, a local protest movement would naturally do everything it could to expand the strength and reach of its message, which usually involved promoting some kind of figurehead. They would develop unique slogans and imagery to get their names out there. They'd organize petitions and gather the names of supporters. Now that governments have the potential ability to spy on citizens, these traditional protest tactics have become a liability. Now hacktivists are using technology to turn the tables and upend the current power dynamic.

The future of Anonymous is tough to call, but its heritage is just as polarizing. It's difficult to determine if Anonymous belongs in the "pro" column or the "con" column on my anonymity checklist. For many, including myself, certain iterations of Anonymous represent the dark side of anonymity, the sort of thing that we're going to have to put up with if we want to have freedom of speech. For others, they're one manifestation of its goodness. Because the meaning of Anonymous is so open to interpretation, it's probably a bit of both.

4

Anonymity Wired

Cypherpunks write code. We know that someone has to write software to defend privacy, and since we can't get privacy unless we all do, we're going to write it. We publish our code so that our fellow Cypherpunks may practice and play with it. Our code is free for all to use, worldwide. We don't much care if you don't approve of the software we write. We know that software can't be destroyed and that a widely dispersed system can't be shut down.
—Eric Hughes

THE HERITAGE of anonymous activism of course goes back far, far beyond the birth of Anonymous. Anonymous is perhaps the most visible manifestation of anonymous activism that the world has seen, but the groundwork had been laid by unsung heroes. The major players in the identity wars are connected through various ideological strands such as privacy, cryptography, and open government. These ideals presage the Web, but beginning in the '80s, one group of brilliant geeks brought them together in vibrant discussion groups, defining the counterculture on the Internet. Everyone from Julian Assange to the random Anon to armchair observers like me owe these mostly forgotten luminaries an immense intellectual debt. For through their eternal resolve and prescient thinking, they defined the way the Internet works more than any businessman on the cover of *Wired*.

From Decoder Rings to Remailers: The Story of Cypherpunk

Up until very recently, cryptography was mostly limited to pen and paper encryption. Cryptography is essentially the science of securing communication from third-party observers. Ancient Egyptians, Hebrews, and Greeks are all known to have employed cryptography to secure information from adversaries. Code making and breaking has had an incalculable impact on the course of world history, especially in the twentieth century. In 1917 the United States discovered the Zimmerman Telegram, an encrypted diplomatic proposal from Germany to Mexico, suggesting that they attack the United States, which eventually resulted in the United States declaring war on Germany, marking its entry into what would come to be known as World War I. And in World War II, the Allies were able to crack Nazi Germany's ciphers created by the Enigma machine. This breakthrough is considered to be the greatest advance in cryptanalysis in over a thousand years.

Modern cryptography is said to have begun in 1949 with Claude Shannon, the author of "Communication Theory of Secrecy Systems," the result of his research and work during World War II. This work established a theoretical framework for cryptography and cryptanalysis. The common theme running through the history of cryptography is that it has only been employed by governments, militaries, and the spies who aid them in order to ensure the safety of sensitive communications.

In the twentieth century, the art of making and breaking

codes developed into a private hobby, perhaps most commonly recognized in popular culture as the basis of Ovaltine's secret decoder rings used in a co-marketing promotion with the *Little Orphan Annie* radio program beginning in 1934. But for the most part, the National Security Agency (NSA) and like government agencies' monopoly on encryption technology stood firm throughout the Cold War. This all changed in the mid-'70s, when two key events changed the landscape of cryptography forever.

The first was the publication of the Data Encryption Standard in the U.S. *Federal Register* in 1975 by a research group at IBM. With the rise of networked computing, private companies began to think of ways to secure electronic communications for financial institutions. For the first time, cryptography was recognized by a government as something needed in the private sector. The NSA approved the Data Encryption Standard in 1977, resulting in an explosion of corporate and academic interest in cryptography.

The second was the advent of public key cryptography in 1976. Before public keys, the sender of information would use a "key" that changed all the letters of a message into gibberish; then the recipient would use the same key to decipher the code. With public key cryptography, both the sender and the recipient have two keys—public and private. Steven Levy, in a *Wired* magazine report on crypto culture, writes:

> If I want to send you a secure letter, I encrypt it with your public key (which I have with your blessing), and send you the cyphertext. You decipher it using your private key. Likewise, if you send a message to me, you can encrypt it with my public key, and I'll switch it back to plaintext with my private key. This principle can also be used for authentication. Only one person

can encrypt text with my private key—me. If you can decode a message with my public key, you know beyond a doubt that it's straight from my machine to yours. The message, in essence, bears my digital signature.

A young computer whiz named Whitfield Diffie, whose passion for cryptography stretched back to childhood, conceived this scheme, which revolutionized the field of cryptography. He'd joined a hacker club at MIT and had become anxious about the responsibility of system administrators, the people who ran computer networks, to give up the information of offending users if served a subpoena. He wanted to figure out a way to secure transmissions of information so they could communicate anonymously. It wasn't easy—most of the accumulated information on cryptography was classified by the NSA. Diffie and Stanford computer scientist Martin Hellman solved the problem in May 1975, with no help or supervision from any government agency.

This discovery brought cryptography out in the open and laid it at the fingertips of genius mathematicians everywhere, especially within academia. From there, the private study of cryptography exploded. First, RSA Data Security commercialized Diffie's discovery in 1977, selling privacy and authentication software to Apple, Microsoft, AT&T, and a host of other firms. Then Philip Zimmermann brought public key encryption to the people.

Zimmermann felt that military-grade cryptography belonged in the hands of the private citizens. In 1991, Zimmerman released PGP, Pretty Good Privacy, based on the algorithms used by RSA, but this time opting to hand out the software for free so that the government couldn't restrict its sale. He posted it to a BBS (bulletin board system), and within days it was being used across the globe. He also opened up the source code, allowing anyone to tinker with the software, point out inefficiencies, and help figure out solutions to improve the product. Representatives from RSA claimed that PGP infringed on their patent, but the service is still in wide use. In fact, several of the old-time crypto geeks I've spoken with while researching this book still include their public keys in their e-mail signatures.

In the 1980s a group of hobbyist cryptographers began to turn their enthusiasm for private communications into a political ideology called "cypherpunk," a derivative of "cyberpunk." Cyberpunk is an aesthetic derived from future noir sci-fi paperbacks like William Gibson's *Neuromancer*, a story about a freewheeling hacker-for-hire who daringly infiltrates security systems and pillages precious data from within. The new term was coined by the activist hacker Jude Milhon who, at an early meeting of the group, quipped, "You guys are just a bunch of cypherpunks." It sounded cool, and it caught on in the press. The moniker stuck. This small band of brilliant geeks decided that it would be dangerous if only the government held the ability to encrypt information and that it was up to them to liberate the power of cryptography as a tool for social change.

The cypherpunks had no leadership, but three men defined the group's ideals. Timothy C. May was a former Intel physicist who codified much of the cypherpunk ideology. Eric Hughes moderated physical meetings. But it was John Gilmore, former Sun Microsystems engineer and activist, who hosted The List, where most of the action among cypherpunks happened. It was a simple mailing list. It wasn't even anonymous. But the back-and-forth discussion, which typically comprised fifty daily messages, connected some of the smartest minds on the Web.

Cypherpunks were antiauthoritarian activists: some were

high-ranking members of influential tech companies, and others were hobbyist hackers. They held meetings, ran mailing lists, and discussed arcane mathematics, computer science, politics, and philosophy, mostly via e-mail. They held individual privacy in the highest esteem, seeing it as the means for those with minority opinions to stand against oppressive majorities (or minorities with power). In the late '80s and early '90s, personal privacy wasn't a topic of public conversation. This was before identity theft, before data mining, and before social networking encouraged the entire world to post their personal information online. Cypherpunks recognized before anyone else that the Internet could become a great tool for either liberty or tyranny, depending on the way the public dealt with privacy concerns.

Eric Hughes wrote "A Cypherpunk's Manifesto" in 1993:

> Privacy is necessary for an open society in the electronic age. Privacy is not secrecy. A private matter is something one doesn't want the whole world to know, but a secret matter is something one doesn't want anybody to know. Privacy is the power to selectively reveal oneself to the world. . . .
>
> Privacy in an open society also requires cryptography. If I say something, I want it heard only by those for whom I intend it. If the content of my speech is available to the world, I have no privacy. To encrypt is to indicate the desire for privacy, and to encrypt with weak cryptography is to indicate not too much desire for privacy. Furthermore, to reveal one's identity with assurance when the default is anonymity requires the cryptographic signature.

Hughes believed that we couldn't expect governments or corporations to grant us privacy, and furthermore he felt that we should anticipate that these powerful organizations would want to restrict privacy, as it would fly in the face of their business models. Channeling Internet pioneer Stewart Brand, he declared, "Information doesn't just want to be free, it longs to be free." Hughes deplored regulations on cryptography because he believed it to be a private act.

The reasoning goes like this: If I want to encrypt something, what business is it of yours? Do you expect me to write all my letters on postcards? Why do we even have envelopes, if not to "encrypt" them away from your view? Besides, laws against cryptography only work for communication within that country's borders. Hughes believed that information intrinsically spreads across the globe, and likewise, the ability to conceal information would as well.

To facilitate the free flow of information, cypherpunks wrote, published, and freely disseminated code in order to build anonymous systems of communication that could not be shut down by any single sovereign government. Out of this miasma came software that provided a foundation for encryption technology, some of which is still used today. The cypherpunks were deeply wary of the "surveillance society" at least a decade before media criticism of post-9/11 security measures made individual privacy a household topic of discussion. The cypherpunks recognized that someone had to rise up to ensure individual privacy, so it may as well be them.

In 1994 prominent cypherpunk Timothy C. May codified the collective's ideals into a massive collection of rhetoric called The Cyphernomicon. He claimed that the group was mostly made up of five hundred to seven hundred students ("they have the time, the Internet accounts"), programmers, and libertarians. Free-market types gravitated toward cypherpunk, and the Internet at large, because its growth was decentralized, almost

anarchic. Ideas are spread through a comparatively merito-
cratic system. It's the most unregulated platform for communication, and therefore provides the libertarian with a model
for the physical civilization he'd like to aim for.

The crossover occurred between programmers, who were
used to creating their own virtual worlds and working with a
free and open system of computing laws, and libertarians, who
cherished the same in a brick-and-mortar sense. Cypherpunk
had no established leadership and no formal agenda. This was
more than an aesthetic choice. The decentralized nature of
the group kept them nimble and helped them to stay under the
government's radar.

May codified four cypherpunk ideals:

- that the government should not be able to snoop into our
  affairs
- that protection of conversations and exchanges is a basic
  right
- that these rights may need to be secured through technology
  rather than through law
- that the power of technology often creates new political
  realities

According to May, everyone uses cryptography, whether
they realize it or not. Keys, signatures, lock combinations,
PIN numbers—all of these are used to keep prying eyes
and hands out, and they do essentially the same things that
computer cryptography does for data. The cypherpunks compared modern wiretapping and surveillance to the system of
ecclesiastical confession that enabled ruling bodies to keep
tabs on the potentially seditious acts of individual subjects
throughout their vast fiefdoms. They believed that the liber-

ation of cryptographic technology was inevitable, that it would spread like a virus, eventually toppling tyrannical governments and empowering the individual. The new age of freedom wouldn't be achieved politically, but through technological evolution, pulling humanity inexorably forward despite the best attempts of bureaucratic meddlers to perpetuate the old ways. Some even believed that the spread of cryptography would bring about a swift collapse of world governments, giving way to digital money, the end of taxation, and Randian ad hoc communities. Any government's attempts to criminalize the pure mathematics of cryptography was seen as tantamount to thought crime. Some of the more libertarian-minded cypherpunks felt that technology could liberate the individual from the "tyranny of the majority" that they believed was the inevitable outcome of democracy. It would allow the individual to decide "which laws are moral and which are bullshit."

The word "play" comes up a lot in cypherpunk rhetoric, which correlates closely with the broader hacker ethic. These geeks, beyond any political aspirations, were tinkerers. In fact, many hardcore cryptographers who participated in cypherpunk discussion groups had little interest in matters of public policy; their minds were consumed with complex mathematical and logic puzzles. Eric Hughes writes:

> Cypherpunks love to practice. They love to play with public key cryptography. They love to play with anonymous and pseudonymous mail forwarding and delivery. . . . They love to play with secure communications of all kinds.

In another manifesto, May predicted that the state would attempt to slow the spread of cryptographic technology under the guise of security concerns, demonizing the practice as a tool for drug dealers, tax evaders, and, worst of all, spies. National secrets would be lost and assassination markets would rise up. He argued that the spread of crypto mirrored that of printing reducing the power of medieval guilds, ecclesiastical control, and government interference of all kinds.

And just as a seemingly minor invention like barbed wire made possible the fencing off of vast ranches and farms, thus altering forever the concepts of land and property rights in the frontier West, so too will the seemingly minor discovery out of an arcane branch of mathematics come to be the wire clippers which dismantle the barbed wire around intellectual property. Arise, you have nothing to lose but your barbed wire fences!

Consider the case of the Clipper Chip, a chipset introduced by the U.S. government in 1993 that would enable telecommunications companies to encrypt voice transmission. The cypherpunks vehemently opposed the legislation backing the chipset, which would introduce a system of encryption that was only breakable by a government actor, since each chip corresponded to a cryptographic "key" that government agencies could use to decrypt data transmitted over a network. One recipient of the cypherpunk mailing list uncovered a serious vulnerability to brute force attacks. But what really put the nail in the coffin was a response by the private crypto community introducing competing cryptographic technologies such as PGP.

The cypherpunks continue to play an active role in anonymity and privacy rights through organizations such as the Electronic Frontier Foundation, but their heroic role in shaping the way the Internet behaves will probably forever be shadowed by flashier accomplishments from CEOs renowned for their consumer electronic gadgets, which is a shame. Would you want to surf the Web on your iPad if every page you visited could be monitored by a man in black?

The Hacker Ethic

After World War II, "Ma Bell" updated their long-distance switching system, basing it on twelve distinct "master tones." When you dialed a number, you would hear a series of tones. This sound was generated by telephone computers sending information to each other to set up the call. The system would produce a combination of two fixed single-frequency tones played simultaneously. Eventually someone figured it out—Joe Engressia, a five-year-old blind kid with an acute sense of hearing and the ability to whistle the tones with perfect pitch. He was whistling out of boredom once when goofing around on the phone and the phone disconnected. So he called up the switch room and asked why. They explained the tone system, which fueled his desire to learn more. Within a few years, a vast network of "phone phreaks," mostly kids, many of them blind, had sprouted up throughout the country. They memorized the clicks and whirs of the system and figured out which combinations of tones could accomplish what.

The ability to manipulate the network and exploit its flaws was intoxicating for the phreakers, but it wasn't about the free phone calls. The early phreakers loved computer systems, figuring out how they worked, where they broke down. Some of them would call the company to give them tips about how to improve their system in order to make phreaking more difficult. This was done out of boredom—it would provide them with a greater challenge—but also out of an almost autistic appreciation for perfect systems.

The phreakers were geeks, before the word was commonly used to describe someone with an obsessive passion for a niche area of interest. Over time they figured out how to "trip" around the world on phone lines, calling up exotic locations and setting up conference calls with one another—all free and, as a result, all illegal. The sense of adventure and discovery must have been euphoric for these kids, especially the blind ones, who might typically be dependent on the help of others to travel to the grocery store. And here they were, virtually gallivanting across the globe through the wires. The ability to control and manipulate a global communications network, when so much of one's life is determined by the decisions of parents and other authority figures, would be attractive to any teenager. It was this illicit thrill that would define the motivations of generations of hackers to come. By the '70s they had figured out how to make machines, dubbed "blue boxes," that would generate exactly the right tones. A couple of teenagers, both named Steve, made the first digital blue box, before going on to found a prominent tech company called Apple.

Their loose organization developed complex etiquette, fanciful nicknames, and even zines. In many cases, anonymity played a crucial role in preserving the integrity of the community. AT&T was understandably disturbed by the phreakers' activities and took pains to figure out how to expose them. They took on monikers like "Captain Crunch," "The Cheshire Cat," "The Midnight Skulker," and "Dr. No," names seemingly cribbed right out of cheap crime novels or comic books. They were fun and flashy but deadly important, considering that messing with the phone system could land one in jail. The phreakers' tendency to adopt noms de guerre directly influenced the pseudonymous nature of the early Internet, prompting the default use of handles and nicknames on early BBSs, especially among hackers who continued to bend the law in order to master computer systems similar to the way the phreakers owned Ma Bell.

Even though most of them had never met in the real world, and didn't even know each other's real names, the community grew. Most remarkably, all of this was done outside of any extant institutional channels. It rose organically through the sheer power of, and enthusiasm for, emerging networking technology.

The phreakers were the first hackers, and with the rise of the home computer, they realized that the hacking possibilities with these new machines were comparatively limitless. A hacker club emerged at MIT, whose members whiled away their days manipulating the mainframe computing systems on campus, figuring out ways to make them perform not just more efficiently, but *differently*. With the rise of networked computing, hacker clubs with names like the Knights of Shadow, Cult of the Dead Cow, Legion of Doom, and Chaos Club popped up throughout the world. *2600: The Hacker Quarterly*, named after the frequency the phreakers used to bust into the phone system, published its first issue in 1984.

As the hacker underground developed, those with more sinister inclinations began to appear in headlines. Some hacker collectives, while not explicitly antisocial, were prankish in nature. The Cult of the Dead Cow declared war on the Church of Scientology a decade before Anonymous got around to it. But for the most part, hackers were about improving systems of all kinds through the open sharing of information. In *Hackers: Heroes of the Computer Revolution*, Steven Levy summarizes the hacker ethic's five general tenets:

- Sharing
- Openness
- Decentralization
- Free access to computers
- World Improvement

Dave Marcus is the director of security research and communications at McAfee Labs, but beyond that, he's a hacker. He spends a lot of time with fellow hackers in a place called "Unallocated Space": eighteen hundred square feet dedicated to geeks exploring systems, analyzing problems, and figuring out solutions. They do hardware hacking. They do lasers. They do robotics and lock picking and carpentry and something called "fire vortexes." It's a sandbox environment for geeks to learn about how stuff works.

Some of the hackers Dave hangs out with are deeply concerned with hacktivism, privacy issues, and legislation that affects the Internet; others couldn't care less:

> It's about answering the question, "Why?" Why does it work like that? Why was it designed like that? What happens when it malfunctions? It could be carpentry, or robotics, or metalsmithing. Hacking is basically an inquisitive way of looking at something and asking, "How can I make this do something it wasn't designed to do? It can do twelve things, how can I make it do that thirteenth thing?"

Chris Wysopal is another one of those hacker–turned–security experts. Currently the CTO of Veracode, a security company that boasts clients like the Federal Aviation Administration and Barclays, Wysopal spent his college years exploring the technology behind computer systems. He got a taste for the hacker world by dialing up BBSs and accessing text files, written by fellow hackers, that explained how phone and computer systems worked.

Wysopal was a part of a hacker space called The L0pht (pronounced: loft) that shared computer manuals and spare parts, which were much harder to come by in the early '90s. Over time The L0pht grew into something closer to a business, with different roles and projects they would work on as teams. Eventually they published security advisories and sold software called L0phtCrack, a password auditing and recovery application.

Because several of the security experts I've spoken with grew up hacking into other people's networks, I asked Wysopal if he could estimate how much of his industry is made up of people who grew up doing the sorts of things that the industry tries to expose.

I wouldn't draw the line at people who say they have accessed networks illegally because you just never know what is truth. Some people tell tall tales and some people are very quiet about any illegal activity. You know a hacker pretty quickly after a few minutes of conversation. They know how to penetrate systems, how to size up the weak spots, and how to operate with stealth. They see technology and they just think differently about it. They understand how to control it and manipulate it in ways never intended by the designers. I would say about 20% of the industry thinks like this. They end up at security consulting companies and in the research teams at software and service providers.

The cybersecurity industry can be described as an arms race between people building and maintaining systems and those who want to break into those systems. Among the latter group, white-hat hackers do it to show off their skill and point out flaws, whereas black-hat hackers do it to steal data or humiliate a victim. The thrill of keeping smart hackers out can be as rewarding as hacking itself. But with Anonymous bringing attention to some of the adventures available to those with enough savviness to figure out how to download the LOIC (not much), the average company now has to contend with the potential of an army of faceless teenagers bearing down on its servers with the fury of a DDoS attack. And according to Wysopal, most of them simply aren't prepared. He says that organizations have been focused on stopping cybercrime and, to some extent, the theft of their intellectual property. They have hardened their financial systems and put access control around secrets.

But malicious hackers don't always target those things. Some, like Anonymous, seek to raise awareness of the injustices they see. This can be done by simply embarrassing the target by exposing any information for which they are custodians, such as customer names and e-mail addresses. Another technique is to simply deface a Web site of little importance that is associated with the target or bring it down through DDoS. All of these techniques send a message that the target is incompetent or not to be trusted.

The more recently politicized hacktivist groups embody the aforementioned elements of the Hacker Ethic as defined by Levy, but is the group sustainable within the broader hacker ecosystem? Will corporate network systems adapt to the threat of low-level mass attacks and infiltrations, or will Anonymous figure out ways to stay one step ahead? Wysopal and many others think they are here to stay.

I think Anonymous can adapt. Their actions have certainly had an effect in raising awareness to the vulnerabilities they have exploited and the security industry is paying attention. There are already solutions to most of the attacks Anonymous uses, it's just that the target companies and organizations don't want to make the tradeoff in cost or flexibility in their computer operations. . . . Additionally when investigations start people go underground and figure out new ways of operating. New people spring up. I don't think Anonymous will just go away.

Computer security is like insurance. It seems really expensive until you need it. If anything, groups like Anonymous will behave as an inoculation against real cyber threats, like the Russian hacker ring that infiltrates your network, steals millions of dollars' worth of data, and sells it on the black market data trade . . . without you even knowing they were in your system. Karim Hijazi, of security contractor Unveillance, which does business with clients in the pharmaceutical and tech industries, among others, told me that the real bad guys will lease botnets for a few weeks, use them to infiltrate a network, pillage millions of dollars' worth of data, then leak a story to the media, telling them that their target is leaking information. Then they'll short sell the stock, making even more money off the resulting media frenzy.

Anonymous, despite causing relatively little damage (with two big exceptions—HBGary and Sony, which managed to survive the attacks with egg on their faces), has caused a great deal of awareness for the need for cybersecurity among companies who deal with large amounts of sensitive data.

Openness, freedom, and meritocracy are highly prized within the hacker community, as seen in the five tenets listed above. It doesn't matter where you're from, where (or if) you went to school, or what you look like. It's all about what you know. For the hackers, computer technology leveled the playing field and enabled them to achieve a sense of social equality within the virtual world that they might otherwise not have enjoyed. One's ability to hack is the ultimate determinant of acceptance within hacker groups. Not all hackers distrust authority, but many do. They see authority figures imposing their will (not to mention their flawed systems) through legislation, excessive policing, closed systems, privacy intrusions, and other forms of bureaucratic bullying. Hackers know they can do it better.

The expansion of hacktivism indicates a natural evolution of the hacker subculture, although I must stress that most skilled hackers look down on Anonymous. They are recognized, rightly, as a handful of computer geniuses who actually know what they're doing, surrounded by a multitude of loud and often sophomoric voices who exist only to cheerlead. However, Anonymous marks the advent of collaborative hacking. As the Internet has become more social, so too has hacktivism. Tools like DDoS require the power of the collective to be effective. Twitter has become a soapbox for hackers who wish to flaunt their epic wins and taunt victims and rivals.

Given all this, it's easy to see why anonymity, or, in most cases, pseudonymity, flourishes within hacker circles. It's not simply because hackers tend toward illicit activities. A pseudonym puts the focus on the act rather than the actor. It reinforces the universal code of meritocracy within the hacker underground. Anonymous as Guy Fawkes mask-wearing hacktivist might not live forever, but his ideals, which match up nicely with the hacker ethic, will.

The Leaksters: Cryptome, Julian Assange, and WikiLeaks

When you think of grassroots media activism, you undoubtedly think of WikiLeaks, the relatively new organization that captured the attention of global media with a series of increasingly shocking information dumps. WikiLeaks has uploaded millions of documents since its launch in 2006, including the notorious Afghan War Diary, the Iraq War Logs, information on Guantánamo Bay detention practices, and one of the most highly publicized leaks of all time—the 2010 release of 251,000 U.S. diplomatic cables.

Assange's ties to the cypherpunks haven't been highly publicized, but in order to fully understand the motivations of this enigmatic figure and the organization he represents, we must first recognize the kiln from which much of his philosophy took form.

Although WikiLeaks has neglected to officially recognize Anonymous as a legitimate ally due to their unorthodox methods, Assange has personally expressed his support of the group. After all, he was a hacktivist in his younger days. In 1989, he hacked into NASA's computer system under the handle "Mendax" using a worm called "WANK" with an Australian group called the International Subversives; this effort was part of an antinuke protest. Assange later claimed that this attack was the origin point of hacktivism. They snuck into various U.S. military Web sites, and eventually the Australian Federal Police got wise when Mendax infiltrated the Canadian telecommunications system. They raided Assange's home, an experience that surely shaped his antiauthoritarian views. He spent some time in a psych ward and even slept outdoors at one point. It wasn't until four years later, in 1996, that the case was settled, resulting in a fine. An e-mail to fellow cypherpunks written by Assange from this period shows his participation in the anti-Scientology movement a decade before Anonymous jumped on board. (In another weird bit of cultural foreshadowing, Assange helped Australian law-enforcement bust a pedophile ring in 1993.)

If Nicole Kidman, Kate Cerberano, John Travolta, Bruce Willis, Demi Moore and Tom Cruise want to spend their fortunes on learning that the earth is in reality the destroyed prison colony of aliens from out of space then so be it. However, money brings power and attracts the corrupt. . . . To the Church the battle isn't won in the courtroom. It is won at the very moment the legal process starts unfolding, creating fear and expense in those the Church opposes. Their worst critic at the moment is not a person, or an organization but a medium— the Internet. The Internet is, by its very nature, a censorship free zone. Censorship, concealment and revelation (for a fee) is the Church's raison d'être.

Assange didn't share many of the right-libertarian, or anarcho-capitalist views of his fellow cypherpunks—his e-mail correspondence displays his many arguments on the subject. But he was vociferous in his support for the group's general freedom-loving goals, ideal of anonymity, and their hatred of the surveillance state and its persecution of so-called victimless crimes. It's not an exaggeration to suggest that Assange saw himself as a Neo-like figure from the film *The Matrix*, sneaking into the bad guys' lairs and bringing about revolution through technology. Assange was far removed from the freewheeling tech scene of Silicon Valley, but he was able to rub shoulders with some of the culture's brightest minds through the raucous cypherpunk list.

Assange's contributions to the list continued into the '00s. When it came time for him to claim the WikiLeaks.org domain, he registered it under two names, John Shipton and John Young, his father and the Webmaster of a site called Cryptome, respectively. On October 3, 2006, Assange sent an e-mail to Young:

You knew me under another name from cypherpunk days. I am involved in a project that you may have feeling for. I will not mention its name yet incase [sic] you feel yu [sic] are not able to be involved.

The project is a mass document leaking project that requires someone with backbone to hold the .org domain registration. We would like that person to be someone who is not privy to the location of the master servers which are otherwise obscured by technical means.

We expect the domain to come under the usual political and legal pressure. The policy for .org requires that registrants details not be false or misleading. It would be an easy play to cancel the domain unless someone were willing to stand up and claim to be the registrant. This person does not need to claim any other knowledge or involvement.

Will you be that person?

Over a decade before Assange founded WikiLeaks, John Young and Deborah Natsios, a pair of militant activists by night and Manhattan-based architects by day, launched Cryptome.org, a platform for the release of sensitive information, basically anything the government doesn't want to go public. Particularly inspired by the cypherpunks, they have uploaded sixty-five thousand files in the last fifteen years.

In 2010 Microsoft successfully shut down Cryptome for a few days by appealing to copyright law, a roundabout way to stifle incriminating information, but one that is increasingly used as IP law grows ever more complex and broad. Cryptome published a series of documents culled from several big companies, including Microsoft. They were essentially tutorials for government agencies explaining how they can appropriately mine user data from various products offered by these companies. Most companies had made these documents public so that their users would know that their information could potentially be handed over to the FBI, for instance. But Microsoft chose to keep their docs secret. Somehow Cryptome got its hands on a copy and uploaded it for the public to see. Microsoft claimed copyright infringement.

Anonymity is essential to Cryptome. People can send in documents using PGP, but Young and Natsios encourage submitters to mail in hard copies, claiming that the postal service remains the most secure way to communicate sensitive information. The FBI, among other agencies, is watching. They warn submitters to be careful in this bit of dark humor on the Cryptome contact page:

> To be sure, if privacy policy means just enough privacy to keep users coming into the spider's Web, then okay, that is the policy used by governments to assure the citizenry it acts in the public interest. As employers act in the interest of their employees, as corporations act in the interest of their stockholders, as religious and educational institutions and professionals act in the interest of their dutiful fee-payers.
>
> Those who promise the most protection are out to skin you alive, those who promise the most privacy are selling your most private possessions.
>
> Cryptome is not trustworthy, and lies. It's a free site, what else could it be but up to no good?

Cryptome has always been just John and Deborah, uploading documents that are sent to them. Meanwhile, WikiLeaks is struggling. It's a not-for-profit organization, but they have fought a costly legal war on several fronts over the last few years, and the accusations of rape against Julian Assange haven't helped matters. As of this writing, he is attempting to appeal to the U.S. Supreme Court against the ruling that he should be extradited to Sweden to face questioning, and has a Stockholm PR agency to deal with the media's focus on his personal troubles. WikiLeaks has also suffered a series of blockades from financial services that have refused to process donations to the organization (which prompted Anonymous to hack MasterCard, Visa, and PayPal in retribution).

It's no accident that Assange's ties to the cypherpunks have not been widely reported by the mainstream media. He hasn't tried to hide them, but he hasn't proudly proclaimed this intellectual heritage. He knew that WikiLeaks' success depended on the organization's ability to generate ideological sympathy among the mainstream channels of political activism, and the punks were simply too radical. Nonetheless, Assange's enthusiasm for speaking truth to power anonymously would steer the course of WikiLeaks.

WikiLeaks has delayed the release of a new platform to ensure the anonymity of whistle-blowers who submit sensitive information. Its electronic submission system has been down for over a year because Assange (also a cypherpunk list subscriber and encryption geek—a massive log of Assange's delightfully snarky e-mails with fellow cypherpunks can be viewed at http://cryptome.org/0001/assange-cpunks.htm) felt that the system could not be trusted. And WikiLeaks has had some trouble protecting the identity of its sources in the past. It's been plagued by infighting. Assange is now trying to raise millions of dollars in donations to keep the enterprise above water.

WikiLeaks is a problematic system. It's vulnerable to attack from "patriotic" rival hackers and terrorists, legal attacks from governments, militaries and corporations, and, perhaps worst of all, it has promoted the celebrity of its leader, Julian Assange, to the point where the focus of the media is no longer on the leaks themselves, but on the dramatic narrative of the organization's most famous face. WikiLeaks' success relied not on its ability to disseminate sensitive information, but from the lucky break they got in Bradley Manning, a U.S. military insider who could have just as easily directly leaked his info anonymously to Pastebin from a random Internet cafe, for instance.

Which is why the February 27, 2012, announcement that WikiLeaks had worked alongside Anonymous hackers to release 5 million internal documents stolen from the private intelligence firm Stratfor made so much sense. WikiLeaks is very dependent on a steady stream of fresh new leaks in order to stay relevant. But it can't employ people to go around the law in order to dig up juicy info.

Meanwhile Anonymous is splintering. Despite rallying thousands of people around its antiestablishment inclinations, its greatest strength is also its greatest weakness. Anonymous can be anything to anyone. And the guy protesting for economic reform in Greece has little in common with the American teen who wants to harass Justin Bieber for lulz. The Anonymous brand has been stretched thin throughout 2011, being used as a banner under which countless, sometimes conflicting, wars are fought. Thus the media has a difficult time wrapping its head around the group. Especially when they claim that they are going to bring down Facebook or the New York Stock Exchange. Anonymous begins to look like the Boy Who Cried Wolf. They lack credibility among the press as a genuine protest movement.

The unofficial partnership between WikiLeaks and Anonymous could prove to be a powerful collaboration. WikiLeaks grants Anonymous a measure of credibility, given their connections with the media and editorial filters. Anonymous offers WikiLeaks their ability to uncover incriminating data, even if it means breaking the law.

As of this writing, Assange has announced that he will run for Australian Senate while he remains under house arrest in the UK.

The Fragmentation of Hacktivism

Even if the Anon/WikiLeaks hybrid proves to be a fruitful relationship, tomorrow's hacktivist may prefer to simply upload leaks directly to the Web and let the media sort it out themselves. Enter Pastebin.

Pastebin calls itself "The #1 Paste Tooll since 2002." It is primarily used by programmers to store and share bits of code, but Pastebin will host any text. While researching for this book, I was surprised to find the complete final manuscript of my last book, *Epic Win for Anonymous*—all 304 pages—available in raw text for anyone to copy and paste onto their computer or e-reader. Pastebin's owner, Jeroen Vader, kindly offered to take down the offending page when I contacted him for an interview. Copyrighted content is probably the least of his worries, as Pastebin has become the platform of choice for Anonymous activists and trolls to post everything from info about upcoming operations to the home addresses and phone numbers of underage girls, who, for whatever reason, have attracted the ire of Anonymous.

This is because Pastebin can be as anonymous as you want it to be, and because you can create a file with a unique, easily shareable URL for your friends, with a single click. The stated goal of the site is simple: "to make it more convenient for people to share large amounts of text online." Vader surely could never have imagined that the platform would be used so extensively by the troll collective, and when I spoke with him, he tended to downplay Pastebin's unintended uses. In his defense, it appears that the amount of programming language that appears on Pastebin dwarfs content that isn't code. The site is also commonly used in tandem with Twitter, allowing people to share messages longer than 140 characters by tweeting a short Pastebin URL.

Vader purchased Pastebin in 2010 when the site was making very little money, not even enough to cover its hosting fees. So even though he purchased the site for a song, it was still a risk. He gradually rolled out new features, like a clipboard and a membership system.

Throughout 2011, LulzSec, Anonymous, and several other trollish hacker groups went on a hacking spree, targeting everyone from Gawker to the FBI, and they all used Pastebin to post their gloating calls to action. But it was the attack on PBS that put LulzSec and Pastebin on the map:

> SET SAIL FOR FAIL! Greetings, Internets. We just finished watching WikiSecrets and were less than impressed. We decided to sail our Lulz Boat over to the PBS servers for further . . . perusing. . . . Anyway, say hello to the insides of the PBS servers, folks. They best watch where they're sailing next time.

By this time, Pastebin was seeing millions of visitors. As of October 2011, the site hosts more than 10 million active pastes. The most popular paste to date is that of an e-mail exchange between Facebook's PR company and a blogger, which featured an accusation that the social network had paid to wage a campaign of misinformation regarding Google's data-mining practices. Due to the massive amount of new pastes each day, it's impossible for Vader to check each one manually. He relies heavily on content filters and a flagging system, which I employed in order to get my book taken down from the site.

According to Vader, "freedom of speech" posts are becoming more popular and often show up in the site's "Trends" section because those posts are so widely shared on Facebook and Twitter. He says he had no idea Pastebin would become the social text-sharing platform it is now, but he's excited because Pastebin is used by a much broader group of people.

Pastebin could represent the future of the info leak economy. The risks are too high to rely on a constant information platform like WikiLeaks or Cryptome. Anonymity can be ensured by leaking directly to a site like Pastebin, and the social nature of the Web will ensure that the information gets passed around, for better or for worse. Anonymous has always repeated the maxim, "You can't kill an idea." Pastebin is such an effective tool for activism (and, well, trolling) because it completely separates the idea from the messenger of the idea.

It's clear that WikiLeaks, while doing much to raise awareness regarding the perceived need for more transparency in government, is not the salvation freedom-lovers have been waiting for. It accomplished much in its run, but its flaws have nearly brought about its ruin. Thankfully, anonymous whistle-blowers have no tools at their disposal to create a massive decentralized leak-sharing system—a system that, unlike WikiLeaks or Cryptome, can't be silenced. Pastebin truly allows hacktivists to form a multiheaded hydra, since it's much easier and faster to throw up five pastes than it is to take down one. And even if Pastebin gets taken down, another site will likely rise to take its place. And even if governments could somehow limit text-submission sites like Pastebin, which, practically speaking, they cannot, this information could be passed around in text files, just like it was in the BBS era.

The Hacktivist Hunters

Some suspect that the golden age of Anonymous-style hacktivism is over, since so many people have been thrown in prison, and the Feds are so closely monitoring the LOIC. Toward the end of summer 2011, things started to fall apart. At DEF CON, a hacker conference attended by over ten thousand, there was an uproarious standoff between two shadowy entities: Anonymous and a duo calling itself "Backtrace Security," a winking reference to the Jessi Slaughter scandal, in which Anonymous trolls targeted a tween girl, and her father desperately declared that he'd "backtraced" the identities of his daughter's tormentors. When Jennifer Emick, a representative of Backtrace, gave a presentation about how she was able to expose high-profile Anons, eventually leading to their arrest, the room descended into chaos.

Emick is a middle-aged mother, not the kind of person you'd imagine going up against Anon, but then again, you wouldn't guess that she was once a proud member either. During the Chanology Days, Emick participated in protests, showing up for weekly picketing outside the church's San Francisco headquarters. At some point, around the HBGary Federal incident, she parted ways with the group, when she recognized that it had been hijacked by a nastier breed of trolls who weren't content to humiliate corrupt organizations, but wanted to ruin lives and put people in serious danger. Emick and Gregg Housh became enemies, and Anons following Housh's marching orders trolled her online and off. Housh claims he had nothing to do with the attacks and that Emick brought them on herself.

Regardless of who hit first (it's probably impossible to know as an outside observer), Emick began to collect information with the goal of serving Anonymous some of its own medicine. She teamed up with Jin Soo Byun, a retired Air Force cryptologist and fellow former-Anon who'd also become disillusioned in the hacktivist group's perceived turn toward increasingly malicious attacks. After learning that Anonymous was planning to attack the Marine Corps base in Quantico, Virginia, in retaliation for the imprisonment of WikiLeaks' biggest source, Bradley Manning, Emick and Byun felt that this response was unreasonably broad and would cause a lot of collateral damage to innocents on the base.

Emick explained how she lures unsuspecting Anons from out of the shadows, often by exploiting petty infighting to gain a foothold among the most active players.

"We joined them to fight a bully, and they became the bully," she says, referring to her initial support of their anti-Scientology efforts. She cites the HBGary incident as the "last straw"; it showed her that Anon had strayed far from its lulzy roots, becoming something overtly malicious.

So Emick and Byun began to sneak around Anonymous IRCs and other gathering places, gradually harvesting evidence, which was surprisingly easy to come by. Then they turned the names over to the FBI, which Emick claims at least partially resulted in the Anon arrests that would follow in fall 2011. Emick claims that a lot of Anons are petty and eager to tattle on their cohorts if they feel they've been snubbed, which allows her to keep tabs on the goings-on of the community.

When we spoke in December 2011, Emick told me that Backtrace Security still works with law enforcement to identify malicious Anons.

The Day the Lulz Died

On March 6, 2012, the FBI announced that it had been working with LulzSec figurehead Sabu for eight months. Now outed as unemployed New Yorker Hector Xavier Monsegur, Sabu's hyperactive Twitter account went dark. The announcement came with a spate of arrests, in which the core group of LulzSec agitators was put behind bars, thanks in part to the betrayal of the turncoat Monsegur. The FBI leveraged a charge of aggravated identity theft and a possible two-year prison sentence in order to compromise Monsegur, but it wasn't easy. A law-enforcement official involved in the sting explained that Monsegur didn't want to abandon his two children, so he turned his back on his comrades.

It turns out that Monsegur pleaded guilty to over ten charges on August 15, 2011, and spent the next eight months cooperating with the FBI, sometimes even working from within their offices, and at home with an FBI-approved laptop. One of Monsegur's FBI handlers explained, "About 90 percent of what you see online is bullshit," meaning that much of Sabu's Twitter posts and other correspondence with the media were engineered directly by the FBI. In addition, the FBI was able to alert government agencies to impending danger before LulzSec struck. They even told Sabu to persuade his followers to stop hacking the CIA because it was "embarrassing."

Sabu was very careful about masking his identity, but all it took was one slipup. He entered an IRC chat room without masking his IP address. Just once, in months and months of activity. That was all it took for the feds to nail him. They watched him for weeks, subpoenaed his Facebook account, dug up stolen credit card numbers, and slowly developed a solid case against the hacktivist. Some have speculated that even though he avoided jail time, he may need to go the full-witness-protection-program route, as he is now the most despised Anon on the planet.

It's likely that Anonymous won't disappear completely, but will instead revert back to its previous methods of nimble, surprise attacks on unsuspecting victims committed by hackers who know what they're doing rather than the widespread social movement that grew out of Anonymous in 2011. Jennifer Emick claims that the LOIC is "useless," since everyone's now afraid to use it. It will be difficult for Anons to work collaboratively now that their ranks are undoubtedly infiltrated by Feds, security contractors, and rival hackers. They will need to figure out ways to remain completely anonymous, unknowable not just to outsiders, but to their fellow hacktivists as well. This is the way the smartest Anons always operated, but hubris is not something the average anon is adept at controlling.

But perhaps the most crushing blow to Anon is its popularity as a news event. There was a time when Anonymous was an underground group operating in the shadows, but with the high-profile hacks of LulzSec and the subsequent rise of Occupy Wall Street and the 99 Percent, Anonymous just isn't as cool and mysterious as it used to be. However, the activity of LulzSec and Anonymous seems to come in waves. Perhaps as it verges on passé, a new generation of young geeks will breathe new life into the group.

Anonymous and LulzSec are by far the most popular manifestations of online anonymity, but they are by no means the most important. I continue coming back to them because they represent the immediate hesitation that comes to mind when we ask ourselves, "Should we allow people to be anonymous on the Internet." Depending on your political leanings, Anonymous sometimes fights for good, but they can also be pure evil. So if we're going to determine if we want the right to anonymity on the Internet, we must analyze its most unpredictable strains before we choose to live with the chaos and indiscriminate spleen of the Anon. In the next chapter, we observe further manifestations of anonymity as a social construct, many of which possess the potential to be far more influential than the headline-grabbing hacktivist group in the long term.

5

The Age of the Anonymous Web

*The deep Web has they're [sic] own . . . language in a way.
People act different, and treat the surface Web as if they're
under when it's the other way around. The surface Web is still
connected to our reality, while the deep Web brings us into a
different world through wires.* —Anonymous

GIVEN RECENT reports about how social media networks
harvest user data, it may seem as though the entire social Web
stands at odds with anonymity. A lot of the old cypherpunks,
for instance, see Facebook as nothing more than the greatest
surveillance tool the CIA has ever come up with. Others recognize the value of social media but carefully consider the information they feed it, instead approaching social media with
the view that it can only turn against you if you give it the right
ammunition. As the public becomes increasingly disturbed by
the creeping transparency of the social Web, the ideal of
anonymity continues to manifest itself in new ways.

Right now it seems like your choices are limited to a binary
decision between "social" and "security," but some techies want
to have it both ways and are trying to give people the opportunity to enjoy the benefits of the social Web without sacrificing
their privacy. The most prominent example is Diaspora, a small

project launched by four geeks based in New York City. They set up a Kickstarter donation page, hoping to raise $10,000, but overshot their goal, eventually garnering $200,641 from an enthusiastic base of supporters looking for a "Facebook-killer."

Social Anonymity

Diaspora is a network of networks consisting of "pods." You can run your own pod, make it public, invite-only, or somewhere in between. It's decentralized, so users run pods on their own home computers or servers. In many ways, Diaspora behaves more like the broader Web rather than an enclosed network like Facebook or Twitter. It uses free, open-source software (GNU Affero General Public License 3.0), so anyone can contribute to the development of the Diaspora platform. Where Facebook acts like a hub, Diaspora allows its users to pass social networking information directly to one another without passing through a server owned by Diaspora.

Privacy concerns are only part of the motivation here. Sometimes people glorify pseudonymity for its intrinsic value. Pseudonymity lowers social risks for speaking one's mind, and therefore a pseudonymous community will expose its participants to a broader spectrum of ideas. Founded by Dmitry Shapiro, the former CTO of MySpace Music, the social network AnyBeat focuses on being the community of choice for people to discuss controversial topics pseudonymously. Shapiro says that people have different social needs. We need to communicate with people we know, which he admits Facebook is pretty good for. But what about the value of open dialogue with strangers who come from strange places and hold strange ideas? Shapiro claims that the reputational properties of pseudonymity will ensure an inclusive, polite environment. As long as you're not spouting hate speech, threats, or pornographic content, you're welcome.

AnyBeat is Shapiro's third venture-backed company since he began his entrepreneurial career in the early '00s. He attributes his love for the Web to the casual conversations with strangers he found through AOL chat rooms in 1995, a decade before journalists started throwing around the term "social Web."

> It was this pseudonymous environment where you could meet complete strangers and have very intimate, open conversations and discuss the kinds of matters that were sometimes difficult to discuss in the physical world. So I spent a lot of time talking about religion, politics and other things that I couldn't talk to my friends about because either they weren't interested in those topics or we just weren't comfortable doing so.

Shapiro eventually moved beyond AOL chat rooms as he discovered the broader Web, but he noticed that our drive to find and share ideas with total strangers continued into the ,00s with the birth of MySpace, which enabled people to foster a persistent, usually pseudonymous, and often traceable identity so that social interactions could be built upon days, months, or even years of previous discussion. And then Facebook came along and killed it. But Shapiro held fast to this idea that humans have an innate need to experience new people and ideas, and the best way to facilitate a flow of new personalities was through pseudonymous social networking, even if many adopt pseudonyms for personality flair rather than for identity protection.

> Humans are social beings. We have a need for new people with fresh perspectives to come into our lives. Unfortunately, as we spend time on Facebook we find that our social graph

gets stagnant because of this discouragement for meeting new people. Lately a bunch of people have been reporting that Facebook numbers are going down on Facebook on some metrics. Some are saying they're bored of Facebook. That's like saying you're bored with email or the phone. I think what people are bored with is their closed social graph. That echo chamber. Human nature dictates this.

Beyond meeting this social need, Shapiro is also passionate about the free-speech element of pseudonymity. He compares free speech on Facebook to free speech in Iran, in that you can say whatever you like, but tomorrow it will be used against you. At AnyBeat people discuss politics, religion, sexuality, psychedelic drugs, anything you wouldn't want people to associate with your real-world identity. Shapiro says that sometimes the discussions get heated and volatile in a way that you'd never see in the real world.

I created an AnyBeat account and explored for a bit. It behaves like Facebook in many ways, but the most immediate departure was an area called the "Public Square," a massive grid of discussion groups built around specific topics. The top-trending discussions dealt with selfishness vs. altruism, guilty pleasures, and an argument about a recent bill that threatens "indefinite detention and martial law in the U.S." Other topics include circumcision and abortion. Definitely not the sort of stuff you'd see popping up in your Facebook news feed. One particularly popular topic was Occupy Wall Street.

Speaking of which, a hyperlocal form of social networking has arisen out of 2011's most important protest movement. The 99 Percent often found itself at odds with the NYPD, and protestors needed to find a way to communicate with one another seamlessly and anonymously. One startupper across the country was surprised to find that a product he'd designed for completely different uses had become the de facto communication platform for some of the protestors. The product was originally envisioned as a way for people to share information at parades, conferences, and universities—places with a high temporary population density—for example, if you're at the South by Southwest conference and you want to send a message to all your friends but don't want to annoy your Twitter followers back home.

Vibe is a Twitter-like iPhone app that allows users to post short-form messages semi-anonymously (messages aren't connected to a social graph, but that's as far as the anonymity goes, technically speaking) at varying levels of geographic magnitude. You can "Whisper" messages, which will send them to other Vibe users within fifty meters. You can also Speak, Shout, or Yell, which will send messages at a five-hundred-meter radius. "Bellowing" will send out a global message. Users can also set a self-destruct timer onto messages so they disappear after fifteen minutes, an hour, all the way up to thirty days.

Vibe's creator, Hazem Sayed, was traveling in California when he first noticed that his product was being used at Occupy Wall Street. Sayed explains that in the early days of the protest there was "mutual discovery" between the protestors and the NYPD "in terms of what was allowed and what wasn't allowed." The rules could change any day. So he flew to New York to check it out.

Earlier that summer, Sayed had set up a projector at nearby Washington Square Park and projected a livestream of Vibe messages on the arch. He also set up an iPad station and allowed passersby to write whatever they were thinking, which would then be displayed for the hundreds of park visitors to see. The messages ranged from open letters to President Obama to criticisms of Bloomberg to personal anecdotes. It was a powerful soapbox.

When he arrived at the OWS protest, Sayed set up a screen to re-create the soapbox and invited people to contribute to the stream using their smartphones. It was a hit. Vibe became an ad hoc communications network that allowed protestors to disseminate not just practical information but also share news with people who weren't at the protest site.

Sayed is quick to point out that users can't know who other users are; because there is no log-in or registration, Vibe doesn't know much about its users. But that doesn't mean users' anonymity is completely secure. If Vibe gets subpoenaed, they can and will turn over IP addresses. To achieve real anonymity, we'll have to go deeper.

Navigating the Deep, Dark Web

I first heard whispers of the deep Web on 4chan. It was often positioned by active users as a place where even the most hardened /b/tard (a nickname for heavy users who hang out on 4chan's "random" board a lot) can find things to shock the system. The deep Web is depicted there as the submerged portion of an iceberg. The Web that we know is the tip, and the massive portion underwater is the deep Web.

"I've just come back from the deep Web," they say, "and look what I found." They share ghastly images and stories, perpetuating the legend of this vast underbelly among underbellies. In these conversations I was led to believe that the deep Web—also called the invisible Web, the darknet, undernet, and several other sinister-sounding names—was home to the sort of content that would get you thrown in jail if it were ever traced back to you. This is true, to an extent, but technically the deep Web comprises anything that isn't crawlable by major search engines like Google. This can mean dynamic URLs that have a long string of parameters that might confuse spiders (the software that "crawls" Web sites to index them for search). Any content that's behind a pay wall or other password authentication is technically included in the deep Web. This would include your e-mail or a pay-to-view newspaper Web site. Any content that lies behind a form, like a survey or poll, often can't be crawled. Some sites purposefully exclude spiders using robots.txt, a file that tells spiders to steer clear of certain Web pages for various legitimate, legal reasons. Pages that are made up of flash content obviously can't be crawled because there's no raw text on the page. So to say that the deep Web is the seedy back alley of the Internet is not entirely accurate.

However, there are parts of the deep Web, accessible only with the use of certain anonymizing software, where baddies hang out. The deep Web is rife with readily available child pornography, terrorist rhetoric, drug and sex trade—all manner of taboo and hateful communication.

One such piece of anonymizing software is called the Onion Router, or Tor, briefly mentioned earlier. Tor reroutes communications coming from your computer around the world across a distributed network of volunteer-run nodes that make up the Tor Network. Tor passes users' traffic through three servers before sending it along to its destination. The network was originally sponsored by the U.S. Office of Naval Research to help military agents abroad bypass firewalls and other "censorware" in countries like China. For this reason, some speculate that the service is routinely monitored by the U.S. government and cannot be trusted.

Technically, Tor is not an anonymizing service so much as an obfuscating one. Tor alone can't keep anyone anonymous; it's merely one item in the smart anon's tool belt. Tor works to anonymize your Internet connection, but can also be applied to specific programs. The most popular program used in tandem with Tor is the Internet browser. The Tor team has built a Firefox extension that applies several "onion-like" layers of obfuscation to data communicated through Firefox. Because Tor routes your traffic around the world, it's not very fast. The more people volunteer to contribute their machines as nodes, the faster Tor will get.

I thought I'd check it out for myself. I downloaded the Tor software, ran the executable file, and installed the software. When I ran the program, within seconds a browser window opened saying, "Congratulations. Your browser is configured to use Tor. Please refer to the Tor Web site for further information about using Tor safely. You are now free to browse the Internet anonymously." I typed in a URL I found on 4chan for an underground deep Web portal called Hidden Wiki, waited about thirty seconds (an eternity in the era of Wideband and FIOS), and a blank page popped up, reading "Looking for Hidden Wiki?" The last two words were blue, indicating a hyperlink, so I clicked it, and up popped a page that looked just like Wikipedia. A sidebar listed the categories that are available to browse: blogs, books, political advocacy, but also drugs and underage erotica. I clicked on a link called "Killer for Hire."

This can't possibly be for real, can it?

> You can call me Slate. All you need to know is that I am well trained and can perform what you need done. I do not need to know your situation with the hit and prefer not to. I'm hired when you want to make sure that the hit doesn't get traced back to you.
>
> - Minimum age for hit is 18.
> - I do not care of the gender of the hit.
> - I do not kill pregnant women.
> - I do not torture the target.

- If hit is a political figure, or is in law enforcement (judges, policemen) there will be an additional fee.
- For an additional fee, I can set it up as a "suicide" or an "accident"
- Hit will take place within 4 weeks.
- Hits outside of the continental US will require an additional 2 weeks of logistics and $5000 in travel fees.
- Once the hit has been made I will message you with a picture or a video and the remaining balance must be paid in full.

A second hit-man site sounds like a Hollywood Russian mafioso wrote it. "It is mutual interest to make everything anonymously," he warns, insisting, "it is not a joke." He gives careful instructions on how to pay through Bitcoins (more on this soon) and reiterates the need for total anonymity on both sides of the transaction. "I don't know you and you don't know me."

If these sites are jokes, they are convincingly conceived. Moving on from the hit men, there are firearm salesmen, hackers for hire ("destroy your enemies!"), an extensive list of Bitcoin traders, illegal gambling sites, white supremacist blogs, whistle-blowing blogs, new world order conspiracy chat rooms, transnational activists, Anonymous operation forums, hacker/phreaker communities, and porn. Oh, the porn. Genital mutilation, necrophilia, zoophilia, watersports, etc. Anything you can imagine is at your fingertips. Which brings us to child pornography. I don't have the guts or inclination to click through to any of these sites, but they're there. And according to people hanging out on 4chan, the stuff available from the Hidden Wiki is only a shallow fraction of what's out there were one prone to dig deeper.

Perhaps the most notorious site available through Tor is the Silk Road, a black market where users can find 340 different illegal drugs: weed, cocaine, heroin—a digital bazaar of pills, tabs, and powders. If I wanted, I could easily order up a smorgasbord of illicit substances and have it delivered within a few days. You have to pay a Bitcoin just to browse the site—its inaccessibility keeps out most looky-loos. The Silk Road doesn't have everything, of course. You won't find any chemicals that are easily weaponized. Sellers promote their wares through a reputation system that isn't much different from the one popularized by eBay. The site only accepts Bitcoins, which, along with mandatory Tor usage, help to ensure the anonymity of buyers and sellers. The Silk Road is one of many hubs for black-market drug trade on the deep Web. It's difficult to tell if the DEA (Drug Enforcement Administration) is going to crack down on this sort of thing, or if we're peering into the future. Anonymizing applications and efforts to pierce such software seem to be progressing apace.

Freenet is another piece of software used to mask identity online. It's been downloaded over 2 million times. Freenet's creator, Ian Clarke, is concerned about the freedom to communicate. He grew up in the south of Ireland in the '80s in a family of Protestants, whom he says are fastidious about staying out of Irish politics. From a young age he was interested in understanding people who held different views.

I remember reading [Sinn Féin leader] Gerry Adams's autobiography at a time when most people considered him a terrorist. I can remember that if he was interviewed on TV they had to use an actor to do a voiceover, because it was illegal to broadcast his actual voice. It wasn't that I agreed with Gerry Adams' beliefs or actions, but I did feel that it was far more productive to understand where people are coming from, to try to step into their shoes, rather than simply demonizing them, which was official government policy at that time. It left me with a strong sense of the futility of censorship, and the value of free communication.

My experience with Freenet's "Linkageddon," one of several directories, is similar to that of Tor's Hidden Wiki. Some of it is innocuous (Bob Chapman's Financial Analysis), some of it funny (Anti–Harry Potter fundamentalists), and some of it horrific (ubiquitous underage porn). Everything looks like an old Geocities page.

Clarke describes Freenet like a decentralized postal system, where people carry each other's mail. For instance, you need to get a letter to your friend Bob in Boston, and your friend Diane is going to Boston for a business trip. You give Diane your letter and have her hand off the letter to James, who happens to live in Bob's neighborhood. The system is decentralized and doesn't rely on any one person more than the others. If Bob can't deliver your letter, you might ask Cheryl, who will be passing through Boston as well. The advantages to this system are such that James doesn't have to know who's sending the letter, and there's no central postal hub that can restrict the delivery of mail through censorship or incapacity. According to research by Freedom House, Freenet is one of the most popular anonymity systems used in China. This was no accident. Clarke says that he intended for the software to be used by activists.

Anonymity for Sale: Anonymizer

But perhaps leaving your anonymity up to a random stranger isn't always the best way. Maybe open-source, distributed software can open users up to threats. So argues Lance Cottrell, previously mentioned as the creator of the Mixmaster anonymous remailer.

Cottrell was working on his Ph.D. in astrophysics in the early '90s at UCSD. He had a workstation at his desk directly connected to the backbone of the Internet where he set up Web sites for his research group. Back then he and his colleagues were thinking a lot about network security because they were worried that other universities might try to acquire their hard-earned research data.

> We were concerned about other universities getting a hold of a list of stars and quasars that we were going to be looking at. So I was very aware of how easy it was to gather data early on, and this coincided with Philip Zimmermann releasing PGP and the Clipper Chip initiative.

At the time, government was saying, "Cryptography is important," but according to Cottrell, it wasn't palatable for certain factions of the government to allow for encryption by passing Clipper Chip legislation without keeping a copy of all the keys. The idea that "bad guys" wouldn't eventually figure out a way to manipulate the Clipper Chip system was ridiculous to Cottrell, and that's how he got involved in anonymous remailers. They wanted to get cryptography into the international public domain before a law was passed to make it illegal, thus neutralizing the effect of the law. From there his involvement moved beyond cryptography to general privacy tools.

He recalls a story from the cypherpunk days:

> The cypherpunks were concerned that the NSA and the whole "Echelon" program suggested that the government was monitoring email and doing keyword searches globally, so a

bunch of people created tools that would automatically insert a random assortment of hot-button keywords into your email. Like bomb, like AK-47, like Uranium 235. If you could overwhelm the filters you could force them to make a human review every email. Human review isn't scalable, so you could easily overwhelm the system.

A frustration with complicated privacy software led Cottrell to develop Anonymizer in the mid-'90s. It's actually quite simple. The Anonymizer client software provides a VPN (virtual private network) connection between the user's computer and the Anonymizer network. When the data gets there, Cottrell's software scrubs off the IP address and gives it one that his company controls, which is changed daily. They have access to a large pool of addresses that they can shuffle people around in. And it's all set up so that when they get subpoenaed (according to Cottrell, it's a question of "when" rather than "if"), there isn't any information to hand over.

> We're not allowed to exercise our judgment about which subpoenas to respond to. I can't say, "No, you're Scientology," or "No, you're just harassing your former employee, I'm not going to respond," or "Oh, here's Al Qaeda, I'm gonna hand over the information." Because refusing to cooperate isn't an option if you want to not be in jail.

Some Anons have expressed concern that any privacy service like Anonymizer that's based in the United States simply has to be colluding with the U.S. government to some degree; otherwise it wouldn't be allowed to exist. Cottrell shrugs these rumors off, claiming that it would be difficult to pass a law encouraging such collusion because of our robust legal history of defense for anonymity.

The U.S. is just about one of the best places in the world to host a service like this because many places in Europe and elsewhere have data retention directives that require you to keep logs and track all this stuff. Even if they required us to keep logs, it still might not affect our users because all of our users are still coming out of it with the same IP address on the same day. I couldn't tell you which of our thousands of users happened to connect to a certain target at a given time.

Cottrell says that the U.S. government may run some nodes, but our intelligence service is tied in knots by our legal system. They're more likely to be run by China. Cottrell explains to me that Web anonymity is often all about trust, and therefore sometimes it's preferable to rely on a company with an outstanding reputation rather than an open source project offering a free solution.

> I personally would never use Tor for anonymity. You're putting a lot of trust in the guy who is operating the system. [The data] is hopping from one server to another, but whoever is running the end node can actually do all sorts of crap to you. Scanners, interceptors, content modifiers . . . there's a lot of things you can do at the last hop. Anyone can set up a Tor node. It's all random, so you have no reason to trust the guy running the nodes you're going through. There's reason to believe that intelligence agencies from almost any country in the world are probably running Tor nodes, as well as organized crime.

Cottrell brings up a recent controversy dealing with a proxy server called HideMyAss, a free browser-based proxy that allegedly allows users to surf the Web anonymously just by typing the URL they wish to visit into an address bar at

HideMyAss .com. Due to its ease of use, the service has been heavily favored by Anons. They also offer a VPN service that encrypts traffic for a fee, currently at $11.52/month. The service, based in the UK, recently turned over its information to American authorities, which led to the arrest of Cody Kretsinger in Phoenix. Going by "recursion," Kretsinger had taken part in the breach of Sony's Web site earlier that spring. In a blog post about the incident, HideMyAss reiterated their policy, while explaining that the illegal activity came to their attention when IRC chat logs indicating Anons were using various proxy services such as HideMyAss were leaked.

Being able to locate abusive users is imperative for the survival of operating a VPN service, if you cannot take action to prevent abuse you risk losing server contracts with the underlying upstream providers that empower your network. Common abuse can be anything from spam to fraud, and more serious cases involve terrorism and child porn.

It's a difference in philosophy, at least business philosophy. Anonymizer takes steps to ensure that no logs are kept but obviously not because Cottrell wants to facilitate evildoers. He simply isn't in the business of being a hall monitor to the Internet.

Our pricing and our positioning is to try to make us less attractive to people who are trying to break the law. It's not in my self-interest to protect lawbreakers. I can't help it but I'd prefer they did it somewhere else.

Cottrell isn't just paying lip service to the idea that he'd prefer freedom fighters to use his service. In March of 1999, he got involved in free-speech efforts in Kosovo.

I knew some people in a human rights organization, and they were saying that there were people reporting on abuses, paramilitary killings and things like that in Kosovo. Milosevic was monitoring to see who wrote the messages and sending in a squad to clean up the guy who reported it. So we were asked to set up a system that would allow for anonymous reporting.

And that's what they did. Under the banner of the Kosovo Privacy Project, they created a completely free Web-based privacy tool that would enable anyone in Kosovo to securely get messages out, bypassing Serbian censorship, and post them to discussion boards without putting themselves at risk. From there, they got involved with the Voice of America in providing some large anticensorship programs in China and Iran that ran for several years. Cottrell says that each service had about one hundred thousand active users in each of those countries.

These initial rumblings of the late '90s foreshadowed the decade of international online activism to come. These efforts would come to a head in an economically and politically turbulent spring in 2011. Some would call it a "social media revolution." Others are convinced that it's a triumph of hacktivism. Regardless of technology's role during the actual protests, there is no doubt that the 2011 unrest in the Middle East was the cresting of a wave that had been propelled by online activism.

Arab Spring: Prototype for Wired Activism

In December 2011 *Time* magazine put "The Protestor" on the cover of its "Person of the Year" issue, citing examples across the globe of people fighting the power, from Athens to New York's Occupy Wall Street. In each of these protest movements, technology played an important role, even if just to magnify the cries of protest throughout global media channels. Nowhere was this cry heard more loudly than the streets of Tahrir. The so-called Arab Spring protests took place throughout the Middle East, but the biggest explosion of mass protest occurred in Cairo, Egypt, under one of the region's most oppressive regimes. Of course, the Mubarak administration owned not just the media but the airwaves, so some activists turned to alternative channels to get the word out.

What do you do, as a reporter in the West, when you're tasked with covering a story that's taking place in a country where a tyrannical government runs the media? If you're Reuters' Anthony De Rosa, you put your ear to the ground and start listening to the streets. I first met De Rosa on Tumblr, where he goes by SoupSoup. If you're on Tumblr, you probably know of him, simply because his general news blog is widely considered to be the community's unofficial newsfeed. He also broadcasts to a Twitter following of twenty-two thousand. With mainly those two platforms, he has positioned himself as one answer to the question, "Where do we go from here?," a question the media's been asking itself since the dawn of the social media era.

De Rosa's office space is flanked by a wall of computer monitors, each tuned to Tweetdeck, a Web application that helps De Rosa monitor, manage, and make sense of thousands of Twitter feeds. To passersby it looks like a wall of text, like the Matrix. But to De Rosa, it's a carefully curated list of the most trustworthy, most consistent reporters and citizen journalists.

I have developed many lists and found good ones created by other people that are focused on specific topics and events that help to focus on specific information. My main feed will bring me news in a more chaotic manner but it's still very valuable because I am using that to monitor the people I have found to be reliable over time. Sometimes I might briefly follow some people in my main feed when a specific event is going on and unfollow them later.

As with any technology, the value that emerges from this system is directly correlated to the time investment put into tweaking it toward specific aims. For De Rosa, the Green Revolution in 2009–2010 represented a turning point in the way mass media would interface with social media.

It was such a eye-opening moment to see so many firsthand reports on the ground, and it was the biggest event I can remember to that date to have most of the news play out, in great detail, over social media.

Since then he has used Twitter to monitor ground reports from citizen journalists, verify information, and find leads and sources. Critics might think that the quality of reportage would decrease when journalists are so reliant on the testimony of an average joe's Twitter feed, but De Rosa dismisses such criticism. He claims that, contrary to conventional wisdom, one actually has more access to evidence with social media than traditional off-line sources. It's easier to follow "digital footprints" and use them as forensic evidence to determine the validity of information coming from certain sources.

The following Arab Spring protests, which began in December 2010, continued to reward reporters who carefully monitored social media channels. De Rosa first observed the protests using traditional sources like Al-Jazeera, but soon found that if he wanted up-to-the-minute coverage, he would have to do his own investigation by watching the situation unfold in real time on Twitter.

According to De Rosa, anonymity played a role in the protests, but by the time the tension swelled to the point where people were out in the streets, the chaos emboldened many to speak openly against the Mubarak regime, despite the danger. But since the initial burst of social media activity coming out of Tahrir Square, the epicenter of the protest, oppressive governments across the Middle East have learned how to monitor chatter on Twitter and Facebook as effectively as Western media junkies.

De Rosa is skeptical about Anonymous's role in the Arab Spring protest.

> I think Anon likes to get involved in anything human rights related even if they try to act like they're only in it for the lulz. The activity I saw with Arab Spring was not nearly as prevalent as Occupy Wall Street, which makes me think they're more invested with OWS because it's a more global movement, while Arab Spring was contained within the Middle East and North Africa.

I spoke with Parvez Sharma, a Muslim filmmaker who has written extensively about the protests for the *Daily Beast* and *Huffington Post*, among others. Sharma shares De Rosa's skepticism that Anonymous played any significant role in furthering the protests, despite claims made primarily by Barrett Brown that Anon's involvement provided crucial tools and information to freedom fighters in Tunisia, Egypt, and elsewhere, specifically by successfully bringing down the Web sites of Egypt's Ministry of Communications and Information Technology, its cabinet, and its Ministry of the Interior.

But Sharma is not just skeptical—he's insulted.

> This is a self-congratulatory clusterfuck of a mostly white social media minority in the U.S. It makes me angry, actually, to

say that [Anonymous] shut down the Web sites. . . . When you're in the middle of a revolution dodging bullets in Tahrir Square, you're not visiting the Web site of the Ministry of Whatever. That Ministry Web site has not had any communication with you through most of your life. The way you access Ministry officials is by standing for hours outside their offices in the heat, trying to bribe someone so you can get something very basic like a phone connection, or electricity or a food subsidy! That's how you deal with these ministries. That's how people have dealt with them for generations. Even if the Mubarak government wants to claim that they have "entered the 21st Century," and set up all these cool Web sites . . . no one's using them! That's great. You brought down these Web sites. It had no impact. There is no relationship between these Web sites and the ordinary man on the street creating the revolution.

In Sharma's view, this attitude is a smaller part of a larger problem, the tendency of Western media cheerleading around the political value of social media. He takes issue with what he calls the "highly misleading" and "problematic" assumption that the idea of social media platforms are creating a digital democracy where everyone is equal. During the Arab Spring protests, commentators from around the Western world claimed, "We are seeing history's first social media revolution." Sharma disagrees.

Saying that, in one of the poorest countries in the Arab Middle East, which does have the highest mobile phone penetration, to assume that all those people are using social media is ridiculous. That this movement was carried forward entirely on the arms of social media is ridiculous. The social media users had never before generationally existed in any kind of communication with the majority of the protestors, who were really very poor people. Yes, for the first time in Egyptian history, young people from rich neighborhoods were standing next to garbage collectors coming from the slum. But that rich young man did not tweet at the garbage collector saying, "Meet me at Tahrir Square."

So there are a few problems with the perception of social media as the force that got the Arab Spring protests off the ground. One is that so few people involved in the protest even have access to the technology. Very few of them have Smartphones, for instance. Another is that according to Sharma, there were fewer than one hundred people consistently tweeting out of Tahrir Square, out of a country of 90 million people.

On the other hand, the blogosphere in Egypt is the richest in the Arab world. Sharma explains that dissent and alternative lifestyles were actively discussed in Egypt, and the Internet was a powerful tool for connecting those who wished to enjoy an alternate identity, to engage in the dual personae of what he calls the "indoor life" in addition to the "outdoor life."

Sharma produced a documentary film called *A Jihad for Love*, which deals with the lives of homosexual Muslims. As early as 2001, Hosni Mubarak carried out the most visible pogrom against gay men in the Middle East, in which fifty-two men were arrested at a nightclub on the Nile. They were later tried in courts as though they were terrorists. Sharma says that prior to this era, Cairo was like the San Francisco of the East. In the following two years, Mubarak carried out a widespread and systematic operation of Internet entrapment, perhaps history's first example of a government acting as moral police on the Internet on a mass scale. Sharma says that during this time, Mubarak's police would engage in entrapment by starting conversations with gay men looking for sex in order to set up stings.

In Iran as well, the Achmadinejad regime has also created a sophisticated monitoring system.

In a country where religion is forced down your throat, how you behave when you step out of your house is policed by the government. For young people, there is a high level of sexual frustration. With a high degree of Internet savvy, there are ways to get passed [sic] firewalls to have a richer life on the Internet—to connect, to have conversations, to have romantic relationships, to hook up for sex, and to be part of dissent. This cannot happen out in the open.

In order to hide from prying eyes, gay men, and later dissenters of all stripes, would turn to anonymity or pseudonymity. Sharma claims that gays have figured out how to access the Web in a way that can't be monitored.

But at the same time, when you're in the middle of a revolution, and every media outlet in the West is saying that the revolution is happening in social media, Hosni Mubarak will then crack down on the Web. He turned off the Internet, like he just flicked a switch—and then there was blackness. That was when there was the highest turnout [in the streets].

Sharma says that the critical mass of people sending messages through Twitter and Facebook were creating a social media revolution, not in Egypt, but on the screens of social media types in the West. But in many cases, the loudest voices were not the most influential movers in the protest movement, simply because it was not safe to speak so loudly against the Mubarak regime. Instead, they found safety in anonymity and pseudonymity. Sharma tells me that as the revolution progressed, there were a significant number of people who were anonymous and had created parallel identities online. They created places to get information, a lot of it in Arabic, unreadable by Western journalists. Eventually the echo chamber in the

West seemed to become more supportive of the protests through the small number of people (fewer than one hundred, according to Sharma) consistently tweeting about it from Tahrir Square. Sharma believes that many of the most important voices moving the revolution forward on the Web did not get the credit they deserve.

One Twitter user called PersianKiwi became a main source of information from the streets of Tehran. He was eventually unmasked, but for a long time he was able to use pseudonymity to spread a message of dissent. Sharma tells me that PersianKiwi was effectively shut down on Facebook after he achieved some notoriety in the West from an article in the *New York Times*, forcing him to set up several different profiles under different names. His enemies, perhaps working for Mubarak, were able to use Facebook's content-flagging system to convince the social network that PersianKiwi was not using his real name—a violation of Facebook's Terms of Service. A similar event occurred with Wael Ghonim, an Egyptian man who created a Facebook page called "We Are All Khaled Said," which called attention to the plight of a man who died after being arrested and beaten by Egyptian police. The Facebook page grew to over one hundred thousand fans, and then it was shut down because Ghonim had used a pseudonym account to create the page.

Due to economic realities, a lot of the communication happening in Cairo was not expressed online, but through the same kind of anonymous pamphleteering that was happening in seventeenth-century England.

"It's about leaflets and pamphlets. Giving people guidelines about what to do when you are hit by tear gas. Revolutions still happen this way," says Sharma.

Jacob Appelbaum of Tor has conducted a number of training sessions in the Middle East so journalists on the ground can anonymously communicate within their protest movement and to the outside world. According to Jacob, people in Egypt used Tor to bypass censorship, enabling them to get news from media outlets outside Egypt that would otherwise be blocked by the Mubarak regime. Appelbaum readily admits that he has no way of knowing how many, as he can only rely on testimony from activists who have admitted to using the service. The Tor team can perform some basic statistical analysis, but mostly they have to rely on what people have openly told them.

Lance Cottrell also suspects that characterizing the Arab Spring protests as the beginning of an exciting new era in cyber activism might be overstating the power of social media. He instead suggests that the dictatorships that survived the Arab Spring will go out and buy the sophisticated equipment necessary to accomplish large-scale monitoring of social networks, if they haven't already.

A study conducted by the Berkman Center for Internet and Society conducted a survey among activist bloggers in twelve languages in eighteen countries. Their sample included 1,080 bloggers referenced by Global Voices Online, a global blog aggregator widely trusted in online freedom-of-speech issues. Of the 244 that responded, they found that 79 percent use circumvention tools, such as Tor, VPNs, or Proxies at least occasionally. Seventy-four percent of respondents believed that they risked detention, arrest, or criminal investigation in posting material critical of their governments online. Fifty-nine percent believed those threats extended to their families.

Harsh economic realities in Egypt and across the Middle East imply that the role of social media in the Arab Spring was perhaps overstated by Western media. However, these protests further solidify the value of anonymous protest in places where freely expressing your unorthodox political or religious views could get one imprisoned or worse.

Little Brother Is Watching

In an episode of NBC's *Parks and Recreation*, libertarian-minded Ron Swanson asks a younger employee why his computer is showing him an ad that says, "Hey Ron Swanson, check out this great offer."

"What the hell?" he asks, dumbfounded at how this machine appears to be snooping into his carefully guarded lifestyle. His employee casually replies that sites share information with other companies when you make a purchase. When he discovers an aerial shot of his homestead on Google Earth, we cut to a shot of Ron furiously chucking his PC into a dumpster out back.

This scene taps into a universal anxiousness. We know we're being followed, but we don't know why, or by whom. We are told that this information gathering will make for a more convenient life, where shopping, entertainment, and romance are intimately tailored to our personal preferences, even if we've never filled out a single questionnaire. We are our clicks. And those clicks live on other people's servers. With every "like," search, and site visit, we are voluntarily painting a picture of ourselves, one that is becoming increasingly difficult to change or control. For now, most of us put up with it and assure ourselves that our unease is simply paranoia. Targeted ads based on user behavior have been around for over a decade. But every once in a while, we're confronted with a particularly cunning ad and wonder, "What the hell?"

I distinctly remember the first time my mother was asked for her home address at a checkout counter.

"Why do you need that?" she reasonably inquired. It was so her name and credit card number could be associated with her address, so the store could send her flyers and coupons for the right products at the right time of the year, based on her purchase behavior. Items she needed, without even realizing it, would materialize at her doorstep. The machines are getting better than our brains at meeting our needs.

Statisticians are in high demand, as we are living in a golden age of behavioral research, where the targeting power of algorithms and cold statistics have usurped the art of creativity in advertising. And it's not just at our desktops, it's everywhere we go. With mobile computing and geolocation data, the amount of data collected will magnify considerably.

Things get creepier when we're shopping online, or even when we're just browsing the Web. Thanks to a clever add-on from Firefox called Collusion, we can see exactly how we're being tracked as we move about the Web. It's simple: Download the add-on and click on the Collusion icon that's always in the corner of your browser window. It opens a tab that generates a real-time graphical representation of the companies that are collecting data from your browsing behavior in real time.

I spent ten minutes going about my daily browsing routine, visiting some social networks, media outlets, and shopping sites. Then I checked the Collusion tab, which has morphed into a screen-filling network of interconnected sites with bland names like AdBrite, AdAdvisor, Trackalyzer, DoubleClick, and WebTrendsLive. Even just simply clicking on a link to CNN sends information to a half dozen of these companies. Some are obvious: Google, Yahoo!, Facebook. But the majority are tiny companies with names that sound made up by a "boring tech company" name generator. These outfits make up a shadow internet that follows you wherever you go. Journalists writing about privacy concerns often put the focus on the big players like Google, but it's really these third parties doing the creepier stuff.

The bottom line is that every move you make on today's Web tells something about yourself. Maybe it's that you love dogs, or that you're looking into chemotherapy alternatives. All these bits of information are worth something to somebody, and when they are put together through the cooperation of these dozens of tracking sites, they paint a detailed picture of you that might shock you in its depth and breadth. You are your clicks.

These companies serve ads based on behavioral, demographic, and geographic data. They give advertisers a choice on where to advertise. The days of big media buys are coming to an end, as an advertiser no longer needs to commit to a big contract with any particular media outlet. They can choose to take out an ad on a site according to incredibly granular criteria. If you're an advertiser who wants to reach highly educated users who are looking to adopt, but you can't afford to take an ad out in *The Economist*, or even Economist.com, you can buy an ad at FreeAdoptionAdvice.biz for pennies, and your ad will only run when someone who's visited Economist.com hits the page. This level of detail is tremendously powerful, and the example above only represents one of the countless tricks that advertisers can pull off with all this data floating around. It's revolutionized the relationship between advertising and media, and has created an arms race for hiring statisticians to figure out better ways to keep people clicking.

I'm on the fence about this sort of data collection. As

someone who partially makes a living writing for the Web, I'm deeply invested in the ability of online publications to monetize their content. A huge portion of the Web industry is dedicated to figuring out how to make people click ads, and targeting based on user behavior is, for now, the best we've got. Users are much more likely to click on ads that have been cleverly targeted. Pay walls, on the other hand, have largely been a failed experiment, with readers practically embracing data collection and retention as an alternative to subscription fees. Web sites are having a hard enough time making a profit as it is. They're desperate and willing to try anything. Do I really want to advocate against the business model that puts food on my table? Right now, data is the fuel that powers the Internet. Without tracking, a lot of my favorite publications would likely be forced to charge me to enjoy their services.

Plus, targeted advertising in some ways is preferable to the clumsy, buckshot-style ads of the pre-Internet era. We're not quite there yet, but it won't be long before I am never confronted with an ad for tampons. That's progression, right?

The obvious question: Does this convenience come at a cost? A lot of activists think so. For now, these companies do not associate the data they gather with your name. But as our identities become more closely linked with our online presences, and as social networks become more averse to anonymous and pseudonymous activity, that may change quickly. And even now, is there really that much practical difference between being tracked under your birth name or 194.66.82.11? The name wall is the last piece of the puzzle, giving hundreds of companies access to a high-definition portrait of you.

Do Not Track

Since Jonathan Mayer was an undergrad, he's split his time between public policy and computer security. One of his projects is the maintenance of DoNotTrack.Us, a Web site that informs people about a browser application built into Firefox that indicates to advertisers that its users don't want to be tracked. It's not just software, it's a push for legislation called the Do Not Track standard.

"I don't care much for the ivory tower—I try to work on projects that actually benefit users. Do Not Track was a concrete way to put users back in control over their online privacy," he says.

The hope is that Do Not Track will be passed in the form of legislation, and advertising companies will have to respect any Web user's decision to block tracking. Congress and the Federal Trade Commission have been considering such legislation since they first proposed a Do Not Track system in December 2010.

Do Not Track signals to Web sites that the user would like to opt out of third-party Web tracking. Mayer tells me that it's roughly equivalent to planting a No Trespassing sign on your browser's lawn. Do Not Track is intended to be a tool for any Web user. Right now approximately 6 percent of Firefox desktop users and 17 percent of Firefox mobile users use the service. Although it comes with Firefox right out of the box, it's not turned on by default. All you need to do is go into Firefox's privacy settings and check a box that says, "Tell Web sites I do not want to be tracked." Done. The option is also available to users of Safari and Internet Explorer.

Whether a tracking company chooses to comply with Do Not

Track is up to them. All the software does is send a signal, a "herald" sent ahead that tells sites "Please don't track my master." But the proponents of Do Not Track hope that federal pressures may one day supplement the existing social pressures that have convinced a handful of tracking companies to play ball.

Obviously many Web companies who rely on advertising revenue are not happy with Do Not Track. They claim that advertising fueled by analytics gathered from site traffic is a primary source of revenue for many Web sites, and Do Not Track legislation would hamstring the Web economy as a result. Mayer suggests that Do Not Track's effect on advertising is marginal, actively restricting only around 4 percent of total online advertising. A second concern is that if Do Not Track were to become legislation, it would only drive tracking underground, since compliance would be difficult to monitor.

The Silent Currency

More than any other aspect of people's everyday lives, exchange has been historically monitored by governments for tax purposes. A government that monitors and controls the flow of currency is a government that, benevolently or not, controls its people. For decades anarchy-minded thinkers have attempted to come up with a system for an alternative currency that can't be watched, manipulated, or taxed by any sovereign entity. In the minds of the most extreme dreamers, an anonymous currency system could upend the traditional nation-state system of government and pave the way for a true libertarian utopia. Others just want to buy some cocaine without getting shot.

The exchange of Bitcoin unites commerce sites on the deep Web. Bitcoin is a decentralized peer-to-peer network (like Bit-

Torrent) that allows people to exchange an electronic currency anonymously. A shadowy figure calling himself Satoshi Nakamoto originally announced his creation on a cryptography mailing list, then released the currency into the world in January 2009.

Nakamoto laid out the philosophy behind Bitcoin in an introductory paper called "Bitcoin: A Peer-to-Peer Electronic Cash System." In this manifesto, Nakamoto claims that the biggest failing of Internet commerce is how greatly it relies on trust between parties engaged in a transaction. When paying in person with cash, trust doesn't matter as much, because you can feel the weight of a shilling in your pocket. Not so when dealing with financial abstractions on the Web.

Traditionally, the trust problem is solved by third-party financial institutions like banks or credit card companies or PayPal, which provide a level of security for buyers and sellers, but at a cost. Nakamoto argues that these services still suffer from a trust-based model. Third parties must mediate disputes, hire bill collectors, maintain cash reserves, and pay employees to manage these processes. All of this is inefficient, but very necessary under current transactional platforms.

That's where Bitcoin comes in. Nakamoto explains:

What is needed is an electronic payment system based on cryptographic proof instead of trust, allowing any two willing parties to transact directly with each other without the need for a trusted third party. Transactions that are computationally impractical to reverse would protect sellers from fraud, and routine escrow mechanisms could easily be implemented to protect buyers . . . we propose a solution . . . using a peer-to-peer distributed timestamp server to generate computational proof of the chronological order of transactions. The system is secure as long as honest nodes collectively control more CPU power than any cooperating group of attacker nodes.

Bitcoin is not completely anonymous because every transaction is publicly logged and anyone can view Bitcoins passing from one "address" to another. The addresses look like strings of numbers, so if I'm careful about preserving my anonymity across every single Bitcoin transaction, then I can't be traced. This is why the illicit online drug, sex, and murder trades now appear to be favoring the currency. Bitcoin experts say that it's a good idea to use a different address with each new transaction so different points along your transaction history can't be connected.

Bitcoin is favored by the same sort of person who gravitates toward the cypherpunk movement because it provides a currency that operates outside any sovereign nation's ability to monitor or control it. Some people have called it a fad, others the future of the free market. Bitcoin builds on decades of cypherpunk experimentation. Preceding anonymous currencies like Ecash, bit gold, RPOW (Reusable Proofs of Work), and b-money caused a stir within geeky communities and fizzled shortly after. Nakamoto explains the system:

> We define an electronic coin as a chain of digital signatures. Each owner transfers the coin to the next by digitally signing a hash of the previous transaction and the public key of the next owner and adding these to the end of the coin. A payee can verify the signatures to verify the chain of ownership.

The historic problem with such a system is that, since the currency is virtual, spenders don't trade the same coin in multiple places. This is called the "double-spend problem," and it's the main reason open currencies have not been widely implemented yet. Digital currency requires some mechanism for keeping track of all the money in the economy to ensure that people aren't "counterfeiting."

The common solution to the double-spend problem is to introduce a central authority, like a mint, that checks all transactions for double spending. But the existence of such an institution would defeat the purpose of having a free and open virtual currency.

Nakamoto solved this problem through the creation of the "block chain." Like torrenting, LOIC, Tor, Wikipedia, and so many other platforms and technologies of the last decade, Bitcoin is driven by the power of individuals across a wide network, pooling their resources for processing power and accountability. Bitcoin users devote their home computers to run a piece of software that collectively simulates a ledger, keeping track of all the transactions. Nakamoto's solution was to harness the power of the crowd through a public time-stamp server, which would publish all Bitcoin transactions for all to see. That way Bitcoin traders can ensure that their incoming currency wasn't already spent somewhere else.

Nakamoto also integrated a "mining" simulation, in which home computers would be used to solve cryptographic puzzles containing transaction data. Users (in this scenario dubbed "miners") who solved the puzzles are rewarded with new Bitcoins. This is meant to simulate the real-world effect of new currency added to the economy through the discovery of precious metals.

By convention, the first transaction in a block is a special transaction that starts a new coin owned by the creator of the block. This adds an incentive for nodes to support the network, and provides a way to initially distribute coins into circulation, since there is no central authority to issue them. The steady addition of a constant of amount of new coins is analogous to gold miners expending resources to add gold to circulation. In our case, it is CPU time and electricity that is expended.

Nakamoto also suggested that his model would encourage people to stay honest. In order to defraud other users, a counterfeiter would theoretically first have to assemble more processing power than all the honest nodes in the system (which would require a lot of expensive servers). By that point, he would have created a powerful mechanism to mine new coins, giving the counterfeiter an incentive to play by the rules and happily contribute to the system rather than manipulating it for his own selfish ends.

All of this might sound like wacky sci-fi, but it caught on—first among libertarians fed up with the Federal Reserve's tendency to inflate the money supply through quantitative easing and to incentivize naughty behavior on Wall Street and in Detroit through a series of massive bailouts. Compared to this farce of a free market, Bitcoins seemed like a safe bet to free-market-leaning prospectors.

In December 2010, a few WikiLeaks enthusiasts began to publicly encourage the organization to accept Bitcoin donations. That way Assange and his colleagues wouldn't be dependent on companies such as PayPal or Visa to process donations. Nakamoto wasn't enthused. He replied:

> The project needs to grow gradually so the software can be strengthened along the way. I make this appeal to WikiLeaks not to try to use bitcoin. Bitcoin is a small beta community in its infancy. You would not stand to get more than pocket change, and the heat you would bring would likely destroy us at this stage.

Shortly thereafter, Nakamoto disappeared, never to be heard from again.

But his creation was just starting to go viral. Bitcoin was suddenly the next big thing among hackers, activists, and geeks of all stripes. It became the de facto currency in the deep Web at places like the Silk Road. The exchange rate rose. And rose. A cottage industry of Bitcoin mining developed as people bought massive computing setups devoted to prospecting. Speculators swooped in. It was a gold rush. Soon small businesses began to offer firearms, alpaca socks, and beef jerky in exchange for Bitcoins.

Hackers and security experts were in awe. One researcher, Dan Kaminsky, renowned for discovering a flaw in the Internet that would allow a hacker to shut down the whole Web, tried to penetrate Bitcoin's code in order to prove its fallibility. He tried everything but was unable to find a foothold that would allow him to compromise the system. He determined that Nakamoto was either a savant with a deep understanding of programming, economics, cryptography, and networking, or that he was a fiction created by a team of experts working together.

Then came the naysayers and the finger waggers. Senator Charles Schumer compared Bitcoin to money-laundering. The U.S. government has a history of punishing those who would create alternatives to the dollar. In 2007, Bernard von Nothaus was charged with "conspiracy against the United States" because he'd been minting his own gold and silver "Liberty Dollars." That same year, a company called e-Gold was found guilty of a similar offense for selling a digital currency redeemable for gold.

Then came the real vultures—hackers. The obvious vulnerability to any digital currency is that it's susceptible to tinkering through the network. As of now, you can't put your Bitcoins in a bank, though some "wallet services" have sprung up, prom-

ising varying levels of security. After a few well-publicized Bitcoin thefts, the price dropped and the community's confidence
in the currency took a big hit. Some suspected that Nakamoto
had orchestrated a massive Ponzi scheme.

Regardless, the flare of popularity surrounding Bitcoin indicates that people want something like Bitcoin to happen. And
when there's a demand, some geek in a garage will figure out
a way to fill it. It might not be called Bitcoin, but an open, distributed currency system seems to be a natural evolution toward anonymous, transnational commercial networks.

Rip It Up and Start Again

After its big leak of U.S. diplomatic cables into the public
domain, WikiLeaks has had some trouble finding a Web hosting company. This is nothing new. Service providers tend to err
on the side of safety when it comes to provocative geopolitical
doings. It's a common frustration among self-described freedom fighters. So far we've examined how anonymous activists
are picking away at different properties of the Web. Some try
to make sure advertisers can't track us. Others aim to put
restrictions on government surveillance. Some build cryptography tools that mask traffic.

The most extreme activists are tired of trying to reform what
they consider to be an irrevocably broken system. As the Internet
becomes a more lucrative ground for corporate interests, the likelihood of censorship of inflammatory content increases. Which is
why some techies are trying to scrap the Internet we have and
build a new one. One of them, a Swedish man named Peter
Sunde, recently tweeted, "Hello all ISPs [Internet Service
Providers] of the world. We're going to add a new competing

root-server since we're tired of ICANN [the Internet Corporation for Assigned Names and Numbers]. Please contact me to help."

Over the last few years, the entertainment industry has been turned upside down, first by Napster, LimeWire, and their ilk. Now, they are being usurped by a peer-to-peer file-sharing scheme that, without a central hub, can't be taken off-line by fiat. It's called BitTorrent. One of the most prominent BitTorrent sites is The Pirate Bay. Its founders, a young and appropriately snotty group of geeks, have somehow managed to keep the site up and running over the last nine years. One of those men is Peter Sunde, who fired off the above salvo on Twitter on November 28, 2010. Sunde is an anticopyright activist based in Sweden, a country where legal loopholes have so far allowed him to escape imprisonment due to his involvement with The Pirate Bay. In a blog post that followed, Sunde wrote, "We haven't organized yet, but are trying to . . . we want the Internet to be uncensored. Having a centralized system that controls our information flow is not acceptable."

And so Sunde and his cohorts want to create a new Internet, one that utilizes the power of decentralized file sharing they perfected with The Pirate Bay. They have no use for ICANN, which oversees the entire Internet's Domain Name System (DNS). When a government decides that a Web site within its borders needs to come down, ICANN makes it happen. The DNS is comprised of thirteen root servers located throughout the world that essentially enable ICANN to shut down access to a site at the touch of a button. Critics have decried ICANN's monopoly for years for being inefficient and under the control of strong special interests. Cypherpunk John Gilmore has been an especially vocal voice of opposition, and PGP creator Philip Zimmermann also expressed disappointment with the organization when I spoke with him:

Something has gone wrong with ICANN. Creation of larger and larger numbers of top-level domains seems to be extortion. I already own PhilipZimmermann.com. Am I compelled to buy PhilipZimmermann.biz and PhilipZimmermann.whatever? I'm not sure the old way was stable in the long term, where everything was controlled by an American institution. Now we've turned over control of these top-level domains to individual countries' governments. And that is going to hurt a lot of people because these governments will do things that are not in the interest of their people. The world is worse off now since that transition.

Sunde hopes to create an alternative to ICANN, one that uses the same peer-to-peer technology that brought the entertainment industry to its knees. Each user will host a portion of a DNS on his own home computer, so that ICANN no longer wields absolute power in the domain space.

Sunde isn't the only one aiming to route around ICANN's control through technology rather than policy change. Another group has created Dot-BIT, which uses proxies and cryptography to move domains around anonymously. It's not quite part of the darknet (it's been called a "dimnet"), but it's not out in the open either like the rest of the Web you and I are familiar with. It has already registered several thousand .bit domains, which can only be accessed by those using a special proxy service.

Dot-BIT is driven by Namecoins, a domain-related "currency" that can be earned or "mined" by contributing your computer's processing power to the network. Users can also purchase Namecoins with cash or Bitcoins. Namecoins are used to anonymously purchase a domain within the Dot-BIT network. This incentivizes participants to help keep the network afloat.

However, the Dot-BIT network, not being a pure darknet, is still vulnerable to censorship by ISPs, who could easily block traffic to .bit domains if compelled to do so. Dot-BIT also lacks the pure anonymity of, say, Tor's .onion network, so it's not the model for a totally free, open Internet that someone like Sunde is looking for.

Liam Young and a group called Tomorrow's Thoughts Today, inspired by uprisings in the Middle East, developed a robotics project involving a fleet of flying drones, each transmitting wireless signals between two hundred and three hundred meters. The group of hovering hotspots is able to swarm into formation and disperse in order to escape detection. They recharge themselves autonomously, flying to a recharge station when low on power.

The effort to create an alternate Internet is still dependant on an extant infrastructure, usually owned by big corporations or governments. So in the event of a complete global network crackdown, unlikely as it may be, these valiant efforts would be for naught. That's why a group of perhaps romantic techies are thinking about alternative infrastructure in the form of satellite networking. Berlin's Chaos Communication Congress and the Hackerspace Global Grid have outlined a project to develop communication satellites that would be put into orbit above the atmosphere. They claim to be aiming for an "uncensorable Internet in space."

No sovereign entity has claimed to own space . . . yet. Of course, speaking in admittedly paranoid hypotheticals, if tyranny became so widespread and comprehensive that it became necessary to turn to satellites, it's likely that such an evil government would figure out a way to shoot them down or otherwise disable them. Regardless, it's an ambitious project, fraught with technical complications. For one thing, low-earth satellites orbit the earth every ninety minutes or so, which means that they can only communicate with a ground station while the satellite is "in view." Stationary satellites would have to be placed farther above the atmosphere, which would create a signal delay, prohibitive for many Web applications. For many hackers involved in the project, free-speech concerns are an auxiliary goal. They just want to explore space and are tired of waiting for decades, relying on underfunded, inefficient space programs to get the job done.

Free the Network

On March 27, 2012, I had the opportunity to attend a private screening of a mini-documentary called *Free the Network*, produced by Vice's tech site, Motherboard.tv. The documentary opens at Occupy Wall Street, first depicted as a wacky, disparate band of activists that developed a curious technocentric bent with the arrival of Anonymous, along with a more or less disorganized faction of hackers who wished to bring about social revolution through technology. The film centers on one of them, a twenty-one-year-old college dropout named Isaac Wilder, the executive director of the Free Network Foundation, which holds the following tenets:

- We are an organization committed to the tenets of free information, free culture, and free society.
- We hold that advances in information technology provide humanity with the ability to effectively face global challenges.
- We contend that our very ability to mobilize, organize, and bring about change depends on our ability to communicate.

- We see that our ability to communicate is purchased from a handful of powerful entities.
- We know that we cannot depend on these entities to support movement away from a status quo from which they are the beneficiaries.
- We believe that access to a free network is a human right, and a necessary tool for environmental and social justice.

Wilder builds communications systems based around Freedom Towers, DIY kits that fit in a suitcase containing everything one would need to set up an ad hoc peer-to-peer network. The instructions are simple: "Plug it in. Press the big green button." It creates a local network that stays up no matter what happens to the wider global Internet. All of this is mostly funded through private donations from family, friends, and fellow revolutionaries. Wilder estimates that the equipment required to assemble a Freedom Tower would have cost over $10,000 as recent as five years ago. Today: $2,000. And it's completely grid independent. That means solar powered batteries, a DC power system, a server, a router, and a suite of powerful software. All contained in a suitcase.

The idea is to build a mesh network, where all computers are nodes that act as transmitters to other computers, in order to decentralize the Internet and remove it from the control of governments and corporations. Wilder argues that if we are ever going to achieve global revolution, we must wrest control of the pipes from multinational telecom companies who would censor or monitor the communication of social revolutionaries.

The documentary depicts the aftermath of a police raid at Zuccotti Park during Occupy Wall Street, specifically rows of laptops that had been smashed in by cops, presumably. Several contributors to the doc speculate that the destruction indicates that the establishment is trying to keep the message down. Maybe the cops are just sick of putting up with a bunch of grungy hippies and this was a method of discouragement rather than an outright conspiracy to destroy information. Either way, it's a dark, dark image, one that makes me immediately sympathize with the need to create information networks that can't be smashed in, let alone censored.

I caught up with Wilder a few days after the screening and asked him where his passion for free networks comes from.

> I went to Cuba. In the summer after my freshman year of college with three of my best friends. I really didn't like it at all. The police state. That people didn't have access to information. It just really got to me. I wrote a science fiction novel about building a free network. I love writing, but realized this would actually be better as science fact than science fiction.

He went back to school and connected with an adviser who pointed him in the direction of the FreedomBox Project, which lit a fire in him.

> I mean, I'd already deleted my Facebook. I was already a Computer Science/Philosophy double major. But I spent one more year in school and then I left to start the foundation.

The FreedomBox is a small device that fits in the palm of your hands. It is a small, Linux-powered computer that plugs directly into a wall with built-in privacy-protected e-mail and chat, and a publishing platform for activists living under tyranny. It's a work in progress, and the team is currently soliciting software packages that will make an ideal FreedomBox.

The project is ambitious, aiming to bring about the collapse of nothing less than China's "Great Firewall."

Wilder says that he'd like to see a burgeoning microwave network in Kansas City, his base of operations and, hopefully, some action in New York and California by the end of 2012. He's quick to reiterate that the technology he wants to see in place is already here.

> [This technology] exists already, all over the world. Athens, Berlin, Spain, Kabul, Nairobi. There are huge microwave networks that do what we're talking about doing. It's not just for the developing world. It's not just cheaper. That it's cheaper means we can do it together. These are hacker collectives providing internet access to people who can't get it any other way because the infrastructure isn't there.

He rattles off a laundry list of hacker projects, citing "unbelievable pioneering work" happening across the globe at the hands of hacker collectives.

Wilder hopes that within five years, a dozen metropolitan areas in the United States will have cooperative networks and the beginnings of distributed Wide Area Networks. He says that satellites are a possibility, but he thinks that they're not the most attractive option due to visibility and tracking problems, as well as high latency. He's more interested in near-space platforms at one hundred thousand feet. These consist of dirigibles, fancy balloons that would float somewhere between Kansas City and Chicago, for instance, connecting the two citywide networks. He says the U.S. Air Force and oil companies have been using these for years.

> This can be a commons. We did it at a small scale at Liberty Park. Next we'll do it for a thousand people. Then for a few hun-

dred thousand people. And ultimately humanity. We'll have a network that we share and operate together for our mutual benefit. I think it'll happen peacefully because the desire for it will be so overwhelming that there will be no way to stop it. This seems like the best way to counter late capitalist hegemony.

The Free Network Foundation isn't interested in pushing for increased government regulation of the Internet. They don't seem to trust the White House any more than they trust AT&T. And so, they rage against the machine by building a new one.

All of the tools examined in this chapter represent a growing appreciation for the ideal of untracked, uncensored communication. For the most part, many of them are fighting for a freer Internet without bothering to petition slow, inefficient governments. They are utilizing technology to route around roadblocks placed by government and corporate bureaucrats through open, distributed systems. When the hand of the establishment clamps down more tightly than these activists can bear, they move to a different platform. When government inflates a currency to the point of worthlessness, they smelt a new one. When corporations band together to restrict a communication platform until it's clunky and useless, they string together a new one. They see themselves as not just building black markets to meet their demands, but constructing an alternate black universe, where the anonymous individual steers his own course, and those who would attempt to control him are left blind, stumbling in the darkness.

6

The Year of the Hacktivist

#OWS Flood New York City. Occupy parks all over the city. Mobilize to Times Square. Union Square. Wall Street. The power of People. RISE UP!   —LulzSec figurehead Sabu

THE YEAR 2011 will be remembered by many cultural historians as the year of Anonymous, the year of LulzSec, or at least the year of the hacktivist. The activities of the various anonymous hacker groups orbiting around Anonymous dominated headlines, especially during the summer, and brought network security and privacy concerns into the public consciousness in a way that we'd never seen before.

The Sony hack was definitely the most damaging in terms of dollars lost to downtime and consumer distrust. Seventy-seven million user accounts were compromised while Sony's customers were left without the ability to play games online (a privilege they'd paid for) for twenty-three days. Compromised information included names, addresses, e-mail addresses, phone numbers, gender, and date of birth in addition to twenty thousand credit card numbers. No one knows for sure who was responsible for this attack. The following month, LulzSec broke into SonyPictures.com and posted fifty thousand password

/e-mail combinations as well as twenty thousand Sony music coupons, which they made freely available to the public in a downloadable .RAR file, costing Sony an estimated $24 billion. Then, in October, Sony announced that its PlayStation Network had been compromised yet again, leading some video-game business commentators to speculate that the attacks on Sony could very well take them out of the console wars, as the great cost of these attacks would put Nintendo and Microsoft in a position to expand their market share in light of ill will toward Sony.

Another Japanese video-game company was targeted in June, Sega Corp, compromising the account information of 1.3 million customers. As in the Sony attack, Sega was forced to bring down its Sega Pass online gaming network. Though no one can say that Anonymous or its related hacktivist groups is responsible, it would seem likely, since Anons have a long history of harassing people within and around the gaming universe. Anonymous's earliest attacks were in online game spaces like EVE Online and Habbo Hotel, universes in which they found they could wreak a lot of havoc without experiencing much real-world blowback. Strangely enough, LulzSec not only denied responsibility but reached out to Sega, offering to track down the hackers because, as one LulzSec member tweeted, "We love the Dreamcast, these people are going down." LulzSec later targeted Nintendo but did not steal any data. They just wanted to teach the video-game giant a lesson: "We didn't mean any harm. Nintendo had already fixed it anyway."

"Tango down—cia.gov—for the lulz," exclaimed one tweet. While the Sony hack probably caused the most financial damage, the attacks that generated the most PR destruction were initiated against the CIA and FBI, two organizations that one would expect to be invulnerable to the attacks from what many assumed at the time (in some cases correctly) to be a bunch of teenage nerds. Now, taking down the CIA public-facing Web site did negligible damage to the operational functioning of the organization. Popular Webcomic "xkcd" illustrated the disparity between what people assumed about this attack and what actually happened, by comparing the hack to an attacker tearing down a poster hung up by the CIA. But still, it was embarrassing, and it generated a lot of buzz for the attacker.

In May, Citigroup discovered a serious security breach, in which hackers were able to access data from over 360,000 credit card accounts, including names, numbers, and contact info. The attack, which only affected 1 percent of Citigroup's customers (still a whopping 21 million), was announced the following month, at which point Citigroup began issuing new cards.

That same month hackers broke into the Lockheed Martin network, breaching the system of the United States' largest weapons manufacturer. Hackers exploited a VPN, a system used by employees to access Lockheed's network remotely. Some experts believe that the attack might have come from China.

Hackers also targeted the International Monetary Fund in May, obtaining contact info and other documents around the same time when the former IMF managing director, Dominique Strauss-Kahn, was arrested in New York for sexual assault. Again, China and Russia are among the chief suspects. Experts suggest that China would be motivated to obtain information about economic aid and policy information for nations in distress due to how China could exploit those transactions in global financial markets.

China was also suspected of employing hackers to steal passwords from hundreds of Google account holders the following month. Google was able to pinpoint the origination point of the hacks in Jinan, the capital of the Shandong province. The Chinese government denied any affiliation with the hackers.

In July Anonymous breached the network of intelligence contractor Booz Allen Hamilton, releasing the data they scraped to the public in a torrent file. The file contained the log-in information of personnel from a variety of government agencies and military branches, like the Department of Homeland Security, the State Department, the Marine Corps, the Air Force, SOCOM (Special Operations Command), and others.

The above examples are just a fraction of what has been made publicly available, and those are likely an even smaller fraction of the total hacking activity in 2011 that's been discovered. Serious hackers are much more careful about covering their tracks than are the hacktivists.

All of these attacks are certainly among the gravest costs of online anonymity. Anyone who wishes to seriously engage with the identity wars must be willing to recognize that there are legitimate costs to supporting the right to remain anonymous. However, as we'll see, security experts tend to agree that the problem lies with buggy code, lazy or negligent network administrators, and bad security practices rather than hacks. One of these experts has good reason to hate anonymous hacktivists, but surprisingly has chosen instead to take responsibility for his failure to keep out baddies and refuses to use anonymity as a scapegoat.

Hacked! One Victim's Story

In June 2011, LulzSec set out to embarrass the FBI by attacking local branches of Infragard, a somewhat shadowy private nonprofit organization partnering with the FBI, which calls itself an "information sharing and analysis effort." This was declared to be a retaliation against NATO's "war" on hackers. They uncovered many instances of Infragard employees using the same passwords in multiple places, a rookie move, especially for an organization partially dedicated to computer security. This was the mistake made by Karim Hijazi, a security veteran who runs Unveillance, a company specializing in data breaches and botnets. Hijazi describes himself as a "hacker wrangler" rather than a pure hacker. With a botnet, hackers can compromise a computer, often with malware or another method of reverse proxy, at which point they gain control of a computer's functions, like keyboard and mouse control, the ability to turn a computer on and off, file sharing, file modification, and other "goofy Hollywood stuff," as Hijazi puts it. The more pertinent botnets are used to harvest confidentials, usually financial data. When Anonymous pools its computer resources together by using the LOIC, it's creating an impromptu botnet, a wonderful tool for automating destruction.

A botnet is a valuable collection of computers operating under the control of a single entity, often used to attack other computers by exploiting the flaws of the communication protocols of the Internet. According to Hijazi, IPv6, an upcoming version of Internet Protocol, will make it more difficult for security companies to deal with botnets. He's skeptical that we'll ever find a way to completely rid ourselves of botnet attacks, since it's fundamentally just an entity calling your computer, and there isn't any way to prevent your computer from recognizing that it's a botnet other than to white-list (or preapprove) other IPs that you wish to allow to communicate with your machine. It's difficult for a computer to discern who is a good visitor and who is a bad visitor. For any customer-facing Web site, white-listing simply isn't an option.

Hijazi says:

> It's no longer the days of hacker on one side breaking into some location around the world. These days you send out a malware payload that will automatically compromise that system and then beacon that information back to server owned or popped by a criminal, and they live millions of miles away. [It's a] hugely powerful tool for anonymity.

And yet, it's not perfect.

"These guys should pray that the FBI finds them first," says Hijazi, explaining that LulzSec affiliates would be lucky to get caught before they step on the toes of actual cyberterrorists, such as the Russian Mafia. When I spoke with him on the phone, he didn't sound angry about the attack, but rather fascinated by the culture that spawns the kind of mentalities that would encourage someone to target a company like his.

On May 25, LulzSec sent Hijazi an anonymous e-mail from a Hushmail address. Hushmail is a Web-based e-mail service that provides PGP encryption. Anons love it, and I've noticed its widespread use across the deep Web during my research. They just wanted to talk.

Hijazi saw LulzSec coming when he noticed a strange amount of activity on his server logs. So he implemented some white-listing, effectively shutting out anyone from his network who hadn't been preapproved. It worked, for a while. Then LulzSec tried to compromise his e-mail environment, an easier task since it wasn't under Hijazi's control, it was under Google's. They were able to get into his Gmail account because he'd used the same password in Gmail that he used to access Infragard.

He noticed that a few of his e-mails had gone from "unread" to "read" and then back to "unread." Someone was snooping around in his Gmail account, and they weren't doing a very discreet job of it. Hijazi then went into Google's Web interface and checked which IPs had accessed his e-mail. Sure enough, he noticed one come in through iPredator, a VPN tool similar to Anonymizer and HideMyAss. Something was definitely up. Hijazi immediately changed his passwords and went through a security checklist in order to play it safe. Then he called the FBI, who told him he'd have to play along with his attackers for a while until he could gather further evidence. So he reached out to LulzSec via chat. They told him they wanted his botnet information. This wasn't a troll. It was extortion.

Unveillance runs a Data Leakage Intelligence Platform based on a network of thousands of "listening posts" spread across the Internet. Say you're a client. When someone tries to get into your system, a beacon from your system sends out a message, which will hopefully be picked up by one of these listening posts. At that point, the platform can (again, hopefully) capture the IP address of the offender. Unveillance tracks spam, viruses, worms, DDoSs, and many more types of abuse using its botnet, but this tool that Unveillance uses for good can just as easily be used to beef up the power of a malicious entity.

Around this time Hijazi began to get a feel for who he was dealing with. The LulzSec members got belligerent, and Hijazi guessed that he was dealing with either a "silly hacker kid" or a group of them. He doesn't know why they targeted him out of the many usernames and passwords they obtained from the Infragard hack, other than a juvenile desire for random destruction. These are not typically the kinds of people that Hijazi is looking out for.

What we're really after is the prototypical seriously hardened criminal, that gun-toting Russian mobster, who can, with a few clicks of a mouse, commit a much more prolific crime without the visceral effect of having to kill someone or rob a bank, and that's incredibly frightening for everyone. It's very appealing to the general public.

Hijazi says that LulzSec members weren't doing a very good job of keeping themselves anonymous. They were banking on privacy laws to protect them. And they were using Tor, which, Hijazi emphasizes, is a *government* proxy, "more or less built by the government to keep tabs on people." He goes so far as to call Tor a "front." Furthermore, several of the LulzSec members registered domains in their own given names. Hijazi chalks this up to hubris.

"Ego got involved and ego got them in trouble."

But will the indiscriminate attacks of Anon-like groups continue in the coming decade? The unanimous response from those I interviewed within the security industry is "yes." Dave Marcus of McAfee told me that the security industry actually thinks about Anonymous and its ilk more than you might think. Some consider the group from a technical aspect, for instance—how to prevent a DDoS attack. Others discuss the group from an operational aspect, trying to figure out what makes the group tick. Dave Marcus, when attending the Hacker Halted conference, witnessed a speaker presenting on Anonymous, who actually logged into an IRC channel in order to chat with random Anons during his presentation.

"It gets talked about a lot," he says. So analysts, commentators, and hackers themselves are all talking about Anonymous, but they all seem to agree that the group, or some hacktivist iteration thereof, will continue to exist indefinitely.

Marcus attributes this fascination not so much to Anonymous's power or influence, but because many of the people who make up the security industry are themselves hackers who espouse some of the countercultural ideals that Anons hold dear.

He argues that hackers will always find a way.

> You can't ever really say that anyone is ever going to make a certain type of attack obsolete. Bad guys are smart. If you were to impose a completely new system, within a relatively short period of time, someone will figure out a way to circumvent that system and find new ways of doing things that aren't necessarily traceable. So by people thinking they can somehow implement a completely trackable system is flawed thinking. It just doesn't work like that. DDoS will always exist in some way.

The problem lies not in authentication, but in buggy, exploitable code.

Karim Hijazi of Unveillance thinks Anonymous is in serious danger (if it hasn't already been fundamentally compromised) of being either knowingly or unknowingly manipulated by an actual cyber threat, such as Russian organized crime. He claims that Anonymous could be a perfect fall guy for more sophisticated hackers, or a great gun-for-hire to use as a misdirection tactic. Say you're a Russian hacker who wants to throw the FBI off your trail. You perform your attack, leave a message in the source code of the victimized site saying, "We are Legion. We do not forgive. We do not forget," and sit back and watch the media go nuts holding Anonymous responsible while you sell the company's data on the black market.

"Anonymous is like a hippie with a gun that's mesmerized by a hair-slicked-back mobster that says he'll fund his operation," he says. The LOIC creates an enormous signal-to-noise ratio. The FBI doesn't have the resources to chase after every fifteen-year-old kid who downloads the software, no matter how serious the offense. They're too busy going after al-Qaeda.

Another likely outcome is that a lot of these members of LulzSec and Anonymous—the smart ones who don't get caught—will one day be grandfathered into the security industry or even work for the U.S. government. Hijazi says that all his employees have been approached by the government at one point or another. It makes sense—governments need creative, agile thinkers who know how to keep up with the latest hacking practices, and they have the money and security to make it worth their while. Corporations are also on the lookout for cybersecurity experts, and will often jump at the chance to give a genius college dropout the opportunity to take off the "black hat" in exchange for a white one. Not only can they offer lucrative salaries, but also the peace of mind of not having to look over their shoulder, knowing that the feds could be just around the corner.

Those hackers who are in it for the love of exploring and mastering systems may be able to find as much enjoyment in figuring out ways to build a better lock, so to speak, as they do in picking the lock. A common theme that I recognized when speaking with security experts was a wry amusement. They would say things along the lines of "You gotta give these bastards credit." Maybe it was my imagination, but some of them seemed to get a real kick out of their antics. I got the feeling that a lot of Anons, at least the ones who are doing the higher-level hacking, are going to grow up in the next few years and end up making a ton of money on the other side, trying to keep Anons out.

On the other hand, Hijazi senses that the sexy appeal of the hacktivist lifestyle may be too strong. For instance, Ryan Cleary, a recently arrested nineteen-year-old member of LulzSec, is now being lionized as a martyr for the cause within hacktivist circles. He went from a nobody to a global celebrity overnight.

> There's a scary self-righteousness and entitlement with this generation. We did consider what's beyond our nose, and this generation seems to be a little bit less . . . it's worrisome. I was following the trial of that Cleary kid. He's probably getting more of a rush being a criminal. It makes more sense for these kids to keep playing around.

Regardless of what you might think about the intentions or results of hacktivists or hackers of any stripe, we must recognize, and wrestle with, the reality of bad guys on the Internet. We can choose to focus on figuring out ways to prevent attacks, whether it's teaching our children how to secure their Facebook accounts, or hiring more corporate network security consultants. Or we can attempt to monitor the Internet so comprehensively that every behavior is traceable to each person's real-world identity. Right now we're trying both.

The tension between total anonymity and total transparency on the Web has taken a particularly tangible form over the last year in what tech journalists are calling the "Nym Wars." When a couple of social networks said that they weren't going to allow people to set up pseudonymous profiles on their networks, the resultant outcry resounded throughout the Web, calling into question not just the pseudonym issue, but a broader discussion of anonymity, identity, and selfhood on the Web.

7

Nym Wars

To you I am neither man nor woman—I come before you as an author only. It is the sole standard by which you have a right to judge me—the sole ground on which I accept your judgment.
    —Charlotte Brönte

BEFORE THE social networking era, geeks who'd been living online for a decade or two had resigned themselves to the idea that anonymity breeds trolls. This reality has never been more concisely expressed than in the Webcomic Penny Arcade's "Greater Internet Fuckwad Theory," which states, "Normal Person + Anonymity + Audience = Total Fuckwad," accompanied by an illustration of a smiling, friendly face transformed by online anonymity into drooling buffoon inexplicably shouting "Shitcock!" The comic has been cited by techies and even academics to make an obvious argument: Anonymity removes the risk of consequence, freeing people to be more carelessly vitriolic online than they ever would be IRL. Anyone who has ever spent five minutes browsing YouTube comment threads can attest to the depths to which discourse can stoop when shrouded in even pseudonymity. For the most part, we netizens have learned to live with it, and even find humor in it. If someone's saying something you don't like, you either block the of-fender or scroll right on by.

But then Facebook brought everyone and their grandma on-line. These folks weren't used to the freewheeling Web, and when Mr. Anonymous called their seven-year-old son a horrible name like the above, they reacted as though a grown man had approached the kid on a street and unleashed the offending expletive in person. Concerned mothers began to write news paper advice columnists, asking about this new thing called "cyberbullying." Something had to be done. For the children.

If You're Not Paying for It, You're the Product

The first e-mail was sent in 1971. Bulletin Board systems fol-lowed seven years later, allowing people to create discussion threads that allowed users to view and reply to other people's comments. Then came browsers, which developed graphical interfaces in 1993 with Mosaic, often credited with populariz-ing the Web. Meanwhile, AOL and several other ISPs began bringing dial-up to thousands of homes for a flat monthly fee. The increase in user-friendliness in the mid-'90s dovetailed with a decrease in cost of access, leading to an explosion of In-ternet use. Personal Web sites were nothing new at this point, but they still required an amount of design and programming knowledge that was prohibitive for the average Internet user.

In 1996, Geocities solved that problem, with simple browser-based tools and templates that created a wide network of fully customizable personal Web pages. Everyone from traveling salesmen to tween gamers began to build their own homes on the Web, places to express themselves and, more important, host communication. In order to increase the exposure of one's Internet presence, one could submit her personal site to any number of directories. This was a clunky way to organize information, too reliant on browsing rather than searching. This was, of course, shortly before Google changed all that (sorry, AltaVista). Powerful search engines made it easier to find what you were looking for, but humanity was still looking for a way to connect. Early social networking sites popped up throughout the late '90s and early '00s. For example, Six Degrees introduced profiles and friend lists. In 2002, Friendster became the first popular social network, with 3 million users. Then came MySpace, Tribe, Classmates.com, Jaiku, and more. In 2004, Facebook burst onto the scene with perceived exclusivity, a focus on real-life friends, and, interestingly, *less* aesthetic customization functionality, which made for a prettier walled garden. Facebook currently serves some 850 million users, having laid waste to all the aforementioned networks within a few years.

This is the story about how a wide percentage of human communication came to be hosted on proprietary platforms and thus subject to an inscrutable tangle of ever-changing terms of service. For the first time in history, our relationships, communications, and cultural output have been placed under the ultimate control of a single corporate entity. Our social lives have proven to be so contingent on the march of technological progression that the company that provides the best business model effectively becomes the public commons, even though it is under private ownership. A single entity has a monopoly on human interaction. This might become problematic.

Back to cyberbullying. Facebook has naturally been the focus of this concern because that's where the kids are. Facebook's solution: Do away with pseudonymity. Everyone uses their real names. That way, if someone's being a jerk, they can take appropriate action (warn/ban the user, loop in the cops, notify the Feds). Facebook's history of real name enforcement is unique among social networks.

2005
"No personal information that you submit to Thefacebook will be available to any user of the Web Site who does not belong to at least one of the groups specified by you in your privacy settings."

The platform was originally open to a select few Ivy League schools. The site's exclusivity encouraged users to be open. After all, everyone else on the site is another brainy achiever. Using one's real name offered enticing networking (and hookup) benefits for an entire generation of upwardly mobile college kids.

2006
"Our default privacy settings limit the information displayed in your profile to your school, your specified local area, and other reasonable community limitations that we tell you about."

When Facebook first launched, the company kept user data within the network and offered solid privacy controls. But then Facebook realized that in order to grow, it would have to do two things. The first was obvious: it would need to open itself up to the rest of the human population. There were only so many Ivy Leaguers. First it would become available to the rest of the academic universe, then the broader public.

2007
"Your name, school name, and profile picture thumbnail will be available in search results across the Facebook network unless you alter your privacy settings."

The second measure was less obvious, and it's what made Facebook the global powerhouse it is. In order to succeed where other social networks failed, Facebook had to become a portal to the rest of the Internet. It would need to figure out a way to become a platform that people used to engage with the broader Web. It would accomplish this through a variety of tools such as Facebook Connect, a set of APIs (application program interfaces) that would, among other things, allow any Web site to authenticate users for commenting, subscriptions, gaming, and more. Facebook Connect turned Facebook into something like an ID card for the Web. The convenience of Connect is unbelievably compelling. And countless Web sites like CNN, Vimeo, and Digg were happy to integrate it. Even anonymity-loving 4chan founder Christopher Poole implemented it in his current startup project, Canvas.

Fall 2009

"Information set to 'everyone' is publicly available information, may be accessed by everyone on the Internet (including people not logged into Facebook), is subject to indexing by third party search engines, may be associated with you outside of Facebook (such as when you visit other sites on the Internet), and may be imported and exported by us and others without privacy limitations. The default privacy setting for certain types of information you post on Facebook is set to 'everyone.' You can review and change the default settings in your privacy settings."

Of course, what this means is that now Facebook knows not only the information you give it on Facebook.com, but every time you allow Facebook Connect to enhance your Web experience on the Internet, Facebook can then harvest that information, parse it, and then sell it to advertisers.

Winter 2009

"Certain categories of information such as your name, profile photo, list of friends and pages you are a fan of, gender, geographic region, and networks you belong to are considered publicly available to everyone, including Facebook-enhanced applications, and therefore do not have privacy settings. You can, however, limit the ability of others to find this information through search using your search privacy settings."

Eight hundred fifty million people are willingly giving Facebook information about themselves on a daily or near-daily basis. Ten years ago, market research companies like Nielson would conduct costly focus groups and hand out surveys that gave comparatively spotty results. Google changed all that, harnessing the ubiquity of their search engine in order to provide advertisers with rich demographic data and simple tools to maximize conversions all in real time. Facebook took the advertising game to the next level because suddenly (and in terms of market share upheaval, it was damn sudden), Facebook had user data that was exponentially richer than that of Google's. See, Facebook's users were telling it what they liked, and who they were, with every click, every status update, every addition to their profiles. Most important, Facebook could offer the rich information found in the interconnectedness of your relationships, also known as the "social graph."

2010

"When you connect with an application or Web site it will have access to General Information about you. The term

*General Information includes your and your friends' names,
profile pictures, gender, user IDs, connections, and any
content shared using the Everyone privacy setting. . . . The
default privacy setting for certain types of information you
post on Facebook is set to 'everyone.' . . . Because it takes
two to connect, your privacy settings only control who can see
the connection on your profile page. If you are uncomfortable
with the connection being publicly available, you should
consider removing (or not making) the connection."*

Being able to tell Pepsi that 80 percent of the people who clicked on an ad are male and 50 percent of that group also play World of Warcraft is lucrative, so it's easy to see why Facebook's privacy policy has gotten increasingly byzantine. They can now describe you to an advertiser in more detail than ever before. The demographic data you provide to them is something that pre-Internet market researchers would never have believed possible.

Facebook has succeeded in their goal of becoming a portal to the rest of the Internet. For many new Web users, Facebook basically *is* the Internet. Where companies used to have to pander to Google in order to find an audience, they now play Facebook's game.

Okay, so Facebook is getting less private, at least by default. If you're smart, you adjust your privacy settings according to your level of comfort. However, most people aren't aware of potential privacy concerns, and the ones who do mostly don't care. From their perspective, Facebook is awesome, and it's free, so one can't complain too much.

Then, in the summer of 2011, came Google+. A lot of people wondered why Google+ would even bother competing with a social giant like Facebook when they are clearly doing so well within the search world and have their hands in so many other experimental pots, like designing cars that drive themselves and making telecommunications companies obsolete.

Google and Facebook rightly know that the company that owns your mind is going to be one that will still be around ten years from now. And they're not the only ones who are operating from this principle. Amazon is currently working with a gold mine of user data culled from its shoppers, and Apple knows all your favorite songs, among other things. The human brain is the next frontier, and each of these Big Four tech companies are scrumming to plant a flag in your gray matter. All of these free or cheap services like iTunes, Amazon Prime, YouTube, Google Maps, and Spotify are based on the hope that the information you leak while using them will one day be valuable to an advertiser that's currently having a bear of a time getting you to click on some dumb banner ad.

Google launched their social network Google+ in June 2011, and tech journalists were excited. As Facebook's Mark Zuckerberg increasingly looked like the next big bad Bill Gates, Google+ promised a privacy-friendly alternative from the "Don't Be Evil" folks. And then the geeks found out that Google+ would require a real name, and they seemed much more serious about it than Facebook who, despite discouraging pseudonyms, had difficulty policing the entirety of their massive network, allowing innumerable pseuds to slip by.

But Google's launch was different than Facebook's. They also released their service as a private beta to a select few, but the geeks who signed up for the beta were a different breed than Zuckerberg's Ivy League pals. Tech-industry professionals possess a rich heritage of pseudonyms, handles, nicknames, and alternate identities. So when Google+ announced that they would be requiring users to set up accounts with their real names, people were surprised and annoyed. And when they started indiscriminately booting people off the network, the outcry resounded across hundreds of blog posts and tweets.

A month after Google announced its identity policy, they clarified that they would give users "a warning and a chance to correct their name in advance of any suspension." Shortly after, a representative announced that Google would implement a four-day grace period between the notice of a violation and a suspension. The outrage continued until October, when Google finally relented, announcing during San Francisco's Web 2.0 Summit that Google is working to include pseudonyms in Google+ at some point in the future.

Of course, Google still wants your real name, but why? Why is this single bit of information so important when social networks can harvest so much other information? Two reasons.

The first, Google wants Google+ to be your portal to the rest of the Internet. More than ever, we're using the Web to find people we know. I don't hand out business cards, I tell people, "Find me on Facebook." When you search for "Cole Stryker" on Google, my Facebook profile will be pretty near the top. People used to make Web pages about themselves. Now they have social network profiles. The Internet is fundamentally about connecting people, and the company that's able to better connect you with the people you're looking for will win.

Second, Google is able to collect a lot of information about you. They have your activity on their mobile operating system, they have your search history, they have your purchase behavior, your likes and dislikes, and your video consumption habits. But without a single name unifying all those bits and pieces of data across all the different platforms Google owns and monitors, it's more difficult for them to paint a picture of who you are. But if they can bring all that together, they can sell your mind to advertisers in unsettling ways.

A legal identity is fundamentally a means of managing exchange between two parties so that one can't get away with cheating the other. Being able to verify that identity is valuable to everyone in commerce. Being the company that all the other companies have to deal with in order to access your identity will bring maximum power and profit. Call it identity brokerage. That's why Google+ wants your real name. If they continue to lose that simple bit of unifying information to Facebook, they've lost.

Where does cyberbullying fit into all this?

It doesn't. If I'm legitimately harassing you on Facebook, I can be just as easily tracked down through this IP address if I'm calling myself Cole Stryker or Fartzilla69. You can also block or mute me. In fact, a person using a pseudonym might be *more* inclined to play nice on a social network since her pseudonym is all she has. She can't rely on her extant social status to bail her out of a jam resulting from her being a jerk, for instance.

There are mechanisms already in place, such as social graph analysis, content filters, proactive moderators, and a customer complaint system, that allows users to flag trolls and suspected SPAMbots. These mechanisms will be much more effective at minimizing bullying, since all a bully or stalker would need to do to trick the real name requirement is sign up as "John Smith." Communities like Reddit, Flickr, Twitter, and LiveJournal prove that civilized discourse can thrive if moderators empower users with the right tools. eBay's feedback system isn't based on real names, and yet millions of users are comfortable conducting business through the site, even when millions of dollars are at stake. If you screw someone over on eBay, everyone you attempt to do business with from that point forward will know about it. Reputation is clearly much more powerful for building accountability and trust than the name your parents gave you when you were born.

I spoke with social media researcher danah boyd (who has been bucking naming conventions for years with her purposefully lowercase name) about the so-called Nym Wars. She argues that bullying is rampant on Facebook because, for the most part, bullying occurs between people who know each other, and the specter of cyberbullying from an unknown stranger is blown out of proportion. Furthermore, online bullying among youth usually pales in comparison to good old face-to-face bullying. She cites a 2007 study by Pew, "Cyberbullying," which found that two-thirds of all teens said that bullying and harassment happens more off-line than online.

Commenting platform Disqus, which powers the comments sections of sites like CNN, Time, IGN, and Fox News, released a study culling data from over one million Web sites that use its hosted service, declaring that "the most important contributors to online communities are those using pseudonyms," with pseudonymous comments comprising over 60 percent of the comments across their rather large sample. Pseudonymous commenters tend to post over six times as frequently. Of course, more comments doesn't always mean better comments, so Disqus attempted to qualify the comments by measuring how they were rated by others in the community. Users can flag Disqus comments as offensive, mark them as SPAM, or "like" them. Comments that received more nested replies were given greater weight. According to the study, more than 60 percent of comments using pseudonyms were "positive," 30 percent "neutral," and only 11 percent "negative." The study also revealed that the rate of positive comments posted by pseudonymous users was higher than those that logged in with Facebook or another identity service under their real names.

All this hullaballoo about cyberbullying and stalking is a red herring. No, this is a turf war, and your brain is just another block of concrete.

"Qu'ils mangent de la brioche."

When I was promoting my last book, I performed an AMA (Ask Me Anything) on Reddit, a popular pseudonymous Web community. I'm a longtime Reddit user, and several people inquired as to why I didn't use my regular Reddit handle, instead opting for a new "throwaway" account under the name "colestryker." After all, at the time I was being harassed by members of Anonymous, who'd uncovered my home address and contacted my family members with idle threats. Why not associate my pseudonym with my real name? It would prove my history of participation in the Reddit community, shield me from accusations of fraud, and endear me to its users. What harm could it do to?

The answer is simple. In this scenario, the secrecy of my pseudonym was more valuable for me to protect. Anonymous already had my birth name, so divulging it gave them no new information. But were they to get their hands on my usual Reddit username, they would be able to pore over years of my comments, in which I describe details about my neighborhood, personal stories about relationships, embarrassing anecdotes, etc. My pseudonym was more authentically me than my birth name.

Mark Zuckerberg recently said, "Having two identities for yourself is an example of a lack of integrity." Easy to say for a white, upper-class, straight male living in one of the freest, most prosperous nations in the world. Who has never had to work under someone else. Who has never had to worry about his children's safety. People who are in such privileged positions probably don't need to rely on anonymity to shield them from a softer, less apparent form of tyranny—the social tyranny of the majority. Anonymity doesn't just protect us from governments and corporations, it shields us from ourselves. Anonymity protects the closeted teenager, the Southern lawyer who's really, *really* into Beanie Babies, the teacher who likes to have a few drinks on Saturday night, the father who's thinking about getting a sex change, and the battered wife who's been told she's overreacting by her family and friends.

Which brings us to Randi Zuckerberg, Mark's sister, who wants anonymity on the Internet to go away. One might interpret such a sentiment as ignorance born from privilege. Like Marie Antoinette uttering the fabled line, "Let them eat cake," Randi Zuckerberg's well-meaning obliviousness to the risks of persistent identity might be recognized as the product of a charmed life. People who rely on anonymity are often most at-risk, the most marginalized by power structures. Those who wish to limit anonymity tend to have good intentions but are dangerously out of touch.

I would love to put her on a panel with a human rights activist who faced imprisonment in Egypt during the Arab Spring protests. I'd imagine the bogeyman of cyberbullying would feel much less threatening.

Toward a New Understanding of Identity

Christopher Poole, 4chan's founder, recently described his vision of identity as prismatic, where you present different facades of your personhood to different people. I couldn't agree more. When I'm jerking around with my dudes, I am a completely different person than when I'm visiting my octogenarian relatives. Call me two-faced, there's nothing disingenuous about it. I present a different version of myself to strangers on Reddit, to my clients, to my sister, and to my dog. Even within Web communities, I'm much more comfortable being snarky and sophomoric on Tumblr than I am on LinkedIn. If I'm playing *Starcraft*, I don't want to use my real name, because then thirteen-year-olds who ganked me inside the game world can come find me on my blog and taunt me there. There's nothing inherently duplicitous about my possession of multiple identities. Managing these different personae is a natural response to the varying social situations we find ourselves in, not just on the Web, but also IRL.

Zuckerberg et al. have either willfully mischaracterized the public perception of identity in order to promote their businesses, or perhaps they're just woefully ignorant of human nature's constancy across history, and that the addition of some new software won't change it. danah boyd is also skeptical.

"Radical transparency" means one thing when you're living in a very privileged environment. It means another thing when you are under surveillance in any aspect of your life. Zuckerberg believes that radical transparency will create an environment where people are more equal. I wish he were right but I don't believe he is. I'm also not willing to accept how many people can and will get hurt in the process.

She says that online identities are less like bodies and more like outfits.

> The anti–multiple identities movement is driven by the notion that an online identity is equivalent to a physical body. But this is not how we experience handles and screennames, login accounts and profiles. Saying that there should only be one identity online is like saying that you should only have one outfit. People change clothes for many reasons. Many people choose different outfits for work and play for good reasons that have nothing to do with being "fake" at work. We put on costumes to have fun in certain situations, not because we're trying to be someone different but because it's fun to dress up every once in a while.

Boyd says that some people like to wear the same outfit, or kinds of outfits anyway, everywhere they go, and that others prefer to put on different looks for different occasions, but that doesn't mean the latter group has something to hide. I asked her if she thinks young people are more concerned about privacy than their parents. She says that the data she's seen suggests that young people care deeply about privacy.

> It's important to remember that privacy is about 1) having agency in a social situation; 2) being able to assert control over that social situation. Any parent knows that young people want privacy in certain situations. . . . But that doesn't mean that they don't want to share. All too often, in the tech world, we focus on the wrong things when we talk about privacy. We focus on access to content but what young people care about is access to meaning.

Ultimately, it's about choice. If you want to use a pseudonym, that's your right. Of course, Facebook isn't public property, so whatever they say goes. For now, it's probably best to protest against trend, but if social networks refuse to recognize the right to pseudonymity, mass exodus might be the only solution.

Government-mandated selfhood can be a prison if you're unlucky enough to be born with the wrong genes, or in the wrong part of the world. It's time for a new understanding of identity.

8

Is Total Anonymity Even Possible?

Good luck! I'm behind seven proxies!
—Traditional Anonymous Taunt

I HAD THE opportunity to take part in a panel discussion in the wake of LulzSec's attacks that dealt with anonymity and the Web. The panel moderator asked me after the talk, "Seriously though, isn't it impossible to be truly anonymous these days? Aren't you fighting a losing battle?"

After the frenzy of cyberattacks in the summer of 2011 came the inevitable crackdown. Dozens of Anons were arrested, both in the United States and abroad, for participating in DDoS and other offenses. It makes one wonder whether, even if Anonymous is sustainable in regards to the whirling organizational chaos it naturally produces, will it survive scrutiny from law enforcement when they cause enough damage to provoke a response?

Thus we come to the broader question: Is it even possible to remain totally anonymous on the Internet? After speaking with several hackers and security experts, the best answer I can provide is, "Yes, but it's *very* hard." Many Anons think they are operating under complete anonymity. Usually, they employ layers of obfuscation that make tracing their steps enough of an annoyance that they'll only be pursued if they really, *really* piss someone off. In most cases, teenage hackers firing up the LOIC, who think it makes them elite badasses, aren't getting away with it because their hacker skills are just that good, but because authorities have to weigh the cost of chasing someone down against the likelihood that capturing their target will yield a reward justifying the effort. Dave Marcus of McAfee suggests that if the Feds decide that the posturing of an Anon on Twitter or somewhere else bears investigation, they'll devote some resources to finding him or her, and they'll probably be successful.

There are many tools available to those who wish to hide their IP address and encrypt data transfers. Below are the categories of anonymizing services, in order of least protection to most protection. IP addresses are allocated by several organizations such as ARIN, the American Registry for Internet Numbers, and saved by your Internet Service Provider and reported back to these organizations. This data is public and can be viewed by anyone at any time by using a WHOIS IP address query (there are several Web sites that provide this service). So for obvious reasons, if you want to remain anonymous, your primary goal is to remove the association between your IP address and your behavior on the Internet. This is not easy, but can be accomplished, at least to a point where it's going to be difficult to find you.

The next problem is data interception. When you visit a Web site, your browser will attempt to resolve the domain name into an IP address by sending a request to the Domain Name System (DNS). The DNS will reply with the appropriate address. It's as though your computer is looking up a number in a phone book. Then it establishes the connection. Once the connection is established, your browser will send additional information, such as the version of the software you're using to browse, your geographic location, and your operating system. If you clicked on a hyperlink to get to a specific site, the site that referred you to your destination will also be logged. Throughout this process, your computer is leaving a paper trail that can be stored in server logs, and then handed over to the authorities or used by malicious hackers. These two core problems represent the biggest threat to your anonymity. There are several ways of solving them. Here they are, in order of easiest and least secure to most difficult/secure.

Fiddling with Your Preferences

This is the sort of thing that everyone, regardless of tech savvy, can do when firing up a new machine, be it a mobile device or a computer.

Block Cookies

Cookies are text files saved by your browser when you visit a Web site. They may contain your log-in info, your preferences, your browser history. They save your computer time when you visit the same Web site often. They also give advertisers information that you might not want them to know. Third-party cookies are sometimes stored on your computer by advertisers that have information-sharing arrangements with Web sites you visit. Browsers give you the option to turn off cookies. Do it.

Private Browsing

Firefox and Chrome now offer Private browsing options that, while turned on, won't save cookies, browsing history, searches, temporary Internet files, or passwords. This option does not protect you from sites logging your traffic.

Sign Out of Social Networks

Google, Facebook, and other networks can track your traffic when Web sites integrate apps such as Facebook Connect. If you want to hide your activity from social networks, you'll want to log out of any and all of them. Avoiding social networks outside of their internal networks is probably a good policy if you wish to remain semi-anonymous.

Get Rid of Browser Extensions, Toolbars, and Other Apps

These pieces of software often record or report your browsing behavior to the sites you visit. Uninstall them. Beware of all plugins and other downloadables.

Disable HTML in E-mail

This will prevent ad-serving companies from using cookies to figure out where you live, when you opened the e-mail and more. Sometimes this data is merely used to send you more finely targeted ads, but if you want to be completely anonymous . . .

Clear History

Browsers give you the option to clear your history. Do it regularly if you think someone might have physical access to your machine.

"Off the Shelf" Tools

Web-Based Redirectors

For Web browsing, a number of Web-based redirectors are available that provide a low level of protection. This includes services like HideMyAss. But not all sites will allow access from a Web-based redirector. Strangely enough, 4chan is one of them. Many secure sites that process financial transactions, such as banking or shopping, will reject requests from redirectors. Another concern, as we saw in the HideMyAss case, is that the redirector itself may be holding logs, and will absolutely turn them over to the authorities if subpoenaed. Some redirectors will use SSL (secure socket layer) encryption between your browser and their site, but not between their site and your destination. Redirectors are the simplest, easiest form of privacy software (no download required), but they have serious limitations.

Encryption Tools

You may wish to make sure no one can read your e-mail or chat. When you click "send" in your e-mail client, typically the software will make a Simple Mail Transfer Protocol (SMTP) connection to your e-mail server. The server will try to deliver the message to your recipient's Internet Service Provider (ISP) mail server, or through an intermediary relay server. Your recipient can then retrieve the mail from his or her ISP using Post Office Protocol (POP) or Internet Message Access Protocol (IMAP). E-mails can be intercepted at any point along this chain. If your mail is stored in an intermediary host, people who work there can hand over your correspondence to the authorities, or if hackers have compromised the security of the mail server, they can then harvest your e-mails that pass through the server. Another concern is network traffic interception, which is done at the ISP level. If your e-mails include hot-button keywords such as "bomb threat" or "kill Obama," that e-mail might be filtered and flagged as suspicious by government agencies. What's more, an e-mail passes along a lot of information about you to the recipient, who might not be someone you can trust. E-mails generally contain time zone, IP address, geolocation, and the version of e-mail software used to send the message. All of this information can be extracted from the e-mail header, which contains the subject, sender, recipient, date, time sent, and time arrived. All of this data could theoretically be used to build a case against you.

And remember, when viewing rich documents that contain HTML, you are also opening yourself up to the same threats, like cookies, that occur when you view Web sites. If you open a message with HTML, and delete it immediately without replying, that message may have contained a hot-linked image, which sends information back to a server, potentially controlled by a malicious entity, that logs when you opened the e-mail along with your IP address and more.

You can set up throwaway Hotmail or Gmail accounts, but if you're really concerned about privacy, you'll want to make sure that your e-mail is encrypted. You can buy software that accomplishes this, or use free open-source PGP encryption. One popular Web-based solution is Hushmail, as previously mentioned. Barrett Brown has used this to solicit information from other Anons on upcoming operations. I've also seen it used on the deep Web by drug dealers and killers for hire. Hushmail is an e-mail server that will encrypt your messages once it receives them, which involves some risk. When one Hushmail user sends a message to another Hushmail user,

Hushmail can't access that information. But according to Hushmail:

> . . . there is no guarantee that we will not be compelled, under an order enforceable under the laws of British Columbia, Canada, to treat a user named in an order differently, and compromise that user's privacy.

If you have the technical know-how, you are much better off using encryption technology on your computer rather than relying on a Web-based platform. There are also a variety of encrypted chat clients on the market, many of which are free and offer varying levels of protection.

Proxy Servers

There is an old 4chan meme that goes like this: "Good luck, I'm behind seven proxies!" which was notoriously uttered by an unknown kid on 4chan who was responding to threats that he would be reported to the authorities. It sounds like ignorant braggadocio, but it's actually based in the accurate perception that the more proxies that lie between you and the recipient of your communication, the less likely you are to be traced. Proxy services include Tor and Freenet. There are different kinds of proxies, some for Web browsing, others for e-mail (remailers are not technically proxies but they function in a similar way). Proxies are protocol dependent, which means that they have to be configured to a specific protocol like "http" or "https." Proxies often use SSH or "secure shell" (a protocol that uses public-key cryptography to secure messages) to encrypt traffic. Successfully anonymizing your traffic through a proxy server is also contingent on software compatibility. Proxies are vulnerable in that you're placing trust on the last guy in the chain. Some proxies are more secure than others in terms of levels of encryption. Proxies are also often set up by malicious hackers looking to harvest the data of unsuspecting noobs. You should avoid "open proxies," which are often honeypots set up by hackers or the feds. Some even exist on virus-infected computers without the owners being aware.

VPN Tunneling

Virtual private networks (VPNs) are more secure than the previous two methods. You may have heard the term when your boss has asked you to work from home over the weekend. Companies use VPN to give remote access to their data networks. They can provide a higher level of data protection as well as anonymity. Users connect to the Internet through an ISP, then use a VPN application, which sets up an encrypted connection. From there, Internet traffic is encrypted and a different IP can be associated with the traffic. This connection can apply to all the programs running on your computer, so that anything you do will be given the same comprehensive encryption and anonymity. VPN protocols (such as PPTP [Point-to-Point Tunneling Protocol], IPsec [Internal Protocol Security], and L2TP [Layer 2 Tunneling Protocol]) use a high level of encryption. Of course, like every other privacy technique, VPN Tunneling is not 100 percent secure.

Further Measures

So you've decided on an anonymizing platform. That covers your connection, but there are many other things to consider, in case the connection fails you. One thing to keep in mind is that if you are using different protocols, you must ensure that you don't accidentally move across platforms, from one protocol to another, or you may give up your identity (e.g., clicking on a hyperlink while chatting or opening an e-mail that auto-downloads hot-linked images from a server controlled by a dubious entity).

Some hackers tend to use VPN services located outside of their home countries, or based in countries that have less robust legal systems that could aid authorities from a Western country. Others say that it's better to go with a VPN service located within the United States, since American privacy laws offer the most protection. It probably depends on what kind of activity you might plan to engage in.

For an extra layer of security, it would be wise to choose a service that accepts Bitcoins or some other form of anonymous currency (even travelers checks), to further obfuscate your connection with the service. Anything that connects you to an anonymizing service is going to limit your deniability.

Always check up on the software you use to make sure you have downloaded the latest security patches. And be careful about the sources from which you download these updates. Hackers caught hundreds of people accessing child pornography by setting up a honeypot disguised to look like a software update site. Just because you're not looking for illicit material doesn't mean it couldn't happen to you.

Deciding which layers of security you want to apply will largely depend on who you fear. If you're worried about your ISP, a VPN might be the best solution. If you are pirating content, a VPN in an obscure foreign nation might be preferable. If you think a person, company, or government is spying on you, a VPN, SSH tunnel, or Tor might be a good bet. If you're totally paranoid that baddies are coming at you from every direction, a combination of all these solutions might be the route for you.

Perhaps the best form of security is to simply access the

Internet from someone else's connection, someone whom you can either trust or, better yet, someone who doesn't know you're there. Beyond that, it's even better to use someone else's machine, or a machine that you purchased with cash. Sabu, one of LulzSec's most vocal members, sent out tweets using a succession of cheap prepaid phones he buys with cash. You might be familiar with this tactic from seeing it employed by drug-dealing gangsters in HBO's *The Wire*.

Let's say you, John Doe, want a high level of anonymity. Netbooks are getting pretty cheap these days, you just bought one for $200, with cash, of course. Since it's brand-new, your netbook contains no personal information, and it certainly hasn't been registered to any software or hardware sites. The next day, you take a bus to the next town and spend an afternoon sipping cappuccinos in a local coffee shop. You sign up for Anonymizer's "Total Net Shield," a package that includes VPN-level encryption, security against data theft, and anonymous surfing. It's currently $99.00 a month. You paid for it with a prepaid Visa card, which you bought with cash, and you signed up with an anonymous Hushmail account. The next day, you go to a different town and find a different coffee shop, and through your new Anonymizer connection, you download Tor, which you use in tandem with Anonymizer. Bear in mind, this is going to slow your connection way, way down. Forget about file sharing. But you're about as anonymous as can be. To pierce your armor, an attacker would have to bypass multiple layers of obfuscation. Individually, these layers wouldn't do you much good, but together, they're going to make it difficult for someone to find you. The coffee shop trick alone should throw off almost anyone. And it can be maintained for a few dollars a day, including the coffee. Just be sure to pay with cash. Happy surfing. Don't do anything I wouldn't do . . .

When all else fails, it's time to DFE (Delete Fucking Everything, in Anonymous-speak). One popular free tool is Darik's Boot and Nuke, or DBAN. The program is designed to completely wipe a hard drive by overwriting the data with pseudorandom numbers, which provides a level of security that simply emptying your Trash or Recycle Bin can't offer.

Another thing that all the security experts I spoke with agreed upon—one simple rule: don't mess up. All it takes is one tiny mistake to provide an attacker, be they the good guys or the bad, with a foothold. You can spend years doing everything right, but one tiny flub can give you away, giving someone with the right skills the opportunity to strike. So yes, it is possible to be anonymous online, but it's not easy, and it requires a lot of technical savvy and eternal vigilance.

9

Is Total Transparency
Even Possible?

*Of all tyrannies a tyranny sincerely exercised for the good of its
victims may be the most oppressive. It may be better to live
under robber barons than under omnipotent moral busybodies.
The robber baron's cruelty may sometimes sleep, his cupidity
may at some point be satiated; but those who torment us for our
own good will torment us without end, for they do so with the
approval of their own conscience.*

—C. S. Lewis, *God in the Dock*
(via Julian Assange's e-mail signature c. 1996–2003)

NOW THAT we know that it is technically possible to be completely anonymous on the Internet as it exists today, the next
question that we must answer lies on the other side of the identity spectrum: Would it be possible to create a completely transparent Web, where anonymity is impossible to achieve. To
some, this would seem a utopian dream free of cyberbullying,
the distribution of child pornography, malicious hacks, and other
unsavory elements of the Web we know. Again, I attempted to
go beyond the loudest voices in this space, the politicians, the
law-enforcement officers, and the starry-eyed startuppers. I

talked to the security experts who grew up trying to break security systems.

Sometimes the question was met with laughter, as though the idea is so preposterous it's not even worth considering. After all, this kind of a Web has been advocated ever since the beginning of the Internet, only to get shot down time and time again by more levelheaded legislators. Even Hillary Clinton, who isn't known for her free-market leanings, vocally expressed an "If it ain't broke, don't fix it" attitude toward federal entities policing the Web.

Lance Cottrell, creator of Anonymizer and the Mixmaster remailer, isn't impressed by legislation proposals.

> I've not heard anything approaching a proposal that didn't seem like it was compromised at birth or would be so cumbersome as to be unusable. Anything that had enough effective identification crosschecks would be impossible to use, and it would still be vulnerable to the hacked computer. Only the honest people will be forced to use this, and the bad guys will run amok. . . . Botnets are so ubiquitous and effective, and will be for the foreseeable future, that an identity requirement would become a tremendous tool for oppressive governments . . . this becomes a huge surveillance apparatus tied up in a nice bow for governments like Syria and China.

The logic here is not unlike that used by those who oppose gun control: if guns are made illegal, then only criminals will have guns, leaving well-meaning folks defenseless. This reasoning is compelling within the identity space, regardless of what you might think about the merits of gun control. Sex trafficking, child pornography, and a host of social ills would continue. If identity were enforced on the Web, we'd see fewer Guy

Fawkes masks, and maybe we'd feel a bit safer, but would we be? The question we have to ask ourselves is: "Does the accessibility of these anonymizing technologies make the world a safer, more equitable, *better* place?" It's difficult to measure, but their abolition certainly wouldn't.

Other hackers, perhaps the more pessimistic of the lot, reacted with stone-faced seriousness. Dave Marcus says:

> If I'm accessing the Internet from my house and you want to trace every key stroke on my machine back to "Dave Marcus," there has to be technology enabling that beyond just the government and corporations. You'd have to have a systemic approach for tracking at that level. You'd have to authenticate access to the Internet. That's a complex system to build. Just because that a communication between two endpoints doesn't necessarily map it to a human being on either one of those endpoints. I'm not saying it's not possible, but it's a complex system.

Even Facebook can't really tell if I'm using my real name. All it requires is a realistic pseudonym (a.k.a. "John Doe" rather than "mOnKeYpRiNcEsS"). In order to truly enforce real names, Facebook will likely need to prove authentication at some higher level than it can provide within its own internal network. And such an authentication process would require a complete reworking of the Internet.

An authentication for the Web: it sounds simple enough. When you bring up your browser, you type in a username and password, then you get access to the Web. Or maybe every computer is assigned a specific ID, and all activity on that machine is associated with the credit card number used to purchase it. Or maybe a thumbprint or retinal scan. There have been calls for such a system from corporate leaders as well as politicians. Mobile phones already operate this way, to an extent. For instance, setting up an account with Apple requires, in some cases, a Social Security identification card, photo ID, and a credit card, all forever associated with the account holder's behavior as they use their phone. As more people begin to use mobile devices as primary browsing and communication platforms, we move closer to a monitored Internet without even noticing.

But to implement an Internet-wide authentication system incorporating all machines connected to the Web would require a billion-dollar global reimagining and rebuilding of the Internet, so comprehensive that it would need to have a different name entirely. The Internet was built from the ground up in a decentralized fashion by pockets of geniuses across the United States working in loose collaboration until basic consensus was reached on various protocols. It was not designed for central control. Internet identity is based on addresses, which may or may not be closely associated with people's real names. It all boils down to this: the Internet, as it exists today, doesn't care if I'm using my real name. The bits and bytes of the Web are indifferent to anyone's will to enforce that association.

Chances are that any proposal that could come close to providing authentication strong enough to associate real names with Internet behavior would be such a privacy concern that civil liberties groups like the Electronic Frontier Foundation and the American Civil Liberties Union would throw themselves on the railroad tracks before allowing such a legislation to pass. And even if it did, it's likely that as always, *hackers will find a way*, just as they found a way to get around encryption crackdowns, just as they found a way to get around copyright. The very existence of botnets shows how malicious actors can store things like child pornography on innocent machines and then use those zombie computers to do their dirty work. Every software system ever created has been hacked, because that's simply how software works. As privacy advocate Bruce Schneier says, "Bits are bits." Bits don't tell you where they came from. They don't tell you not to copy them. They're just information.

In the spring of 2011, the U.S. federal government introduced the final version of its National Strategy for Trusted Identities in Cyberspace, which proposes a new identity ecosystem that would facilitate commerce by implementing agreed-upon standards for identity authentication. Its advocates insist that it's not designed to create a national identity system, but rather allows individuals to choose from a number of privacy-preserving identity providers.

According to Jonathan Mayer, who watches cyberlaw like a hawk because of his involvement in the Do Not Track project, the field is packed with myriad actors, issues, and incentives. It's difficult to predict how individual pieces of legislation will develop. Statutory law is in a holding pattern, especially with the current Congress. The courts tend to dismiss privacy and security class action suits for lack of economic significance. As far as the federal level goes, Mayer is skeptical that laws like PROTECT IP (Preventing Real Online Threats to Economic Creativity and Theft of Intellectual Property—politicians love overwrought acronyms) will pass given growing bipartisan opposition. He looks forward to computer security legislation deliberation in the spring of 2012, but concrete proposals are not yet on the table. Anything like NSTIC (National Strategy for Trusted Identities in Cyberspace) or an "Internet kill switch" is going to have trouble passing.

To lay the blame for malicious attacks on anonymity fails to get at the root of the problem: security standards that haven't kept apace with infiltration technology. Mayer continues his hypothetical scenario:

> The sad state of software security—the latest DHS weekly bulletin alone identified over 40 "high severity" vulnerabilities —is what enables malicious users to exploit the Internet's indelible capacity for anonymity. Modifying the prior hypothetical, suppose Alice now wants to spam, phish, denial of service (DoS) attack, or hack Charlie. After compromising Bob's computer with malicious software (malware), Alice can send emails, host Web sites, and launch DDoS attacks from it; Charlie knows Bob is apparently misbehaving, but has no means of discovering Alice's role. Nearly all spam, phishing, and DoS attacks are now perpetrated with networks of compromised computers like Bob's (botnets). At the writing of a July 2009 private sector report, just five botnets sourced nearly 75% of spam. Worse yet, botnets are increasingly self-perpetuating: spam and phishing Web sites propagate malware that compromises new computers for the botnet.

According to Mayer, the policy community and the White House are already trending toward the acceptance of Internet anonymity and instead focusing on software security and authentication.

Karim Hijazi of Unveillance thinks that international privacy laws will prevent any single government from locking down the Internet with an authentication wall, and speculates that the geopolitical landscape would have to experience serious disruption in order for such a far-reaching change to the Internet to take place. Furthermore, he suspects that it just won't be worth the money for governments to engage in such comprehensive policing of the Web.

He draws an analogy from the film *Fight Club*, in which the antiheroic protagonist explains that he's a recall coordinator for a major automobile manufacturer. It's his job to run analysis on the rate of failure and compare the cost of an out-of-court settlement with the cost of a recall. If it costs the company less to do the settlement, they'll leave dangerous cars out in the field even if it means that people will die because the numbers just don't add up. Hijazi says that the government policing the Web can follow a similar pattern.

> Unless you really put teeth on [a punishment] and say, "You're going to go to prison," and apply horrendous ramifications (normally it's a fine), typically the fine is lower than what it costs to "fix" the problem. So in my opinion it's an economic failure. It isn't economically viable for a government body to lock down the Web to prevent anonymity.

But Hijazi says the government is certainly keeping an eye on the behavior of groups like Anonymous, for instance. The infiltration of HBGary definitely "raised a lot of eyebrows within the government," according to Hijazi. HBGary Federal's Aaron Barr was involved in some "tremendously grey ops," which he says feeds into the "tin-foil hat wearers looking for a conspiracy." The HBGary attack got attention because of the embarrassment factor. It made the establishment look foolish.

Meanwhile, the corporate sector seems to be more aware of the threats now than ever before. Anonymous's antics, as harmless as they often are, have generated widespread awareness of the need for cyber security. Says Hijazi:

> It's horrific, the amount of data on corporate America and governments—most of its financial stuff—that's out there. It's

just a matter of time before someone says, "Hey look at these petabytes of information." Most people can't believe the amount of info we're able to gather without even having access to their network.

Ultimately any identification system would have to rely on "higher" forms of identification, like driver's licenses, credit cards, national IDs, or passports—and God knows those are never lost, stolen, forged, or otherwise abused! Even if a thumbprint or retinal scanner system were to be developed, it could potentially lead to some sort of black market for compromised machines. The point is that trying to solve a problem at the system access level is impossible unless you don't mind seriously hamstringing the rest of legitimate behavior on the Web. Clamping down on identity simply makes identity theft more tantalizing to criminals and reduces the value of the Web for the rest of us.

Stanford's Jonathan Mayer presents a second object lesson to present his view of anonymity's inevitability:

> Consider our hypothetical of three Internet users: Alice, Bob, and Charlie. If Alice wants to communicate anonymously with Charlie, she may relay her messages through Bob. While Charlie knows Bob is an intermediary, Charlie does not know with whom he is ultimately communicating. For even greater anonymity Alice can pass her messages through multiple Bobs, and by applying cryptography she can ensure no individual Bob can piece together that she is communicating with Charlie. This basic approach to anonymity is remarkable in its independence of the Internet's design: it only requires that some Bob(s) can and do run intermediary software. Even on an Internet where users could verify each other's identity this means of anonymity would remain viable.

The hacker finds closed systems to be claustrophobic. And hackers for hire will potentially have greater opportunity than ever to wreak havoc if they can find a hole within the new system, just as "criminals with guns" might have in a society with strict gun control. Only in this case, the cops won't have guns either. A system like this would have to rely on fear and an aggressive police state. It might look like China, for instance.

10

Faces of Anonymity

WHEN SOME people think about anonymity they imagine a mysterious figure lurking in the darkness who is probably up to no good. Allow me to introduce you to a gallery of case studies, people who have chosen to take on the cloak of anonymity or pseudonymity for innumerable reasons that have nothing to do with cowardice nor crime. They were kind enough to speak with me, sometimes using their real names, because they care deeply about the right to express themselves freely without fear. We begin with a lighthearted example, primarily to show that one doesn't have to be living under totalitarianism to find value in namelessness.

The Comedienne

A few years ago a woman started a blog, coketalk.tumblr.com, an unfiltered look at LA hedonism. It was fresh, funny, and intriguing, mostly because no one knew who was writing it. Along with the Tumblr platform, the blog grew in popularity over the next few years, eventually expanding as a brand into advice and style blogs and leading to a regular gig for its author as an advice columnist for the *Daily*, the iPad's digital newspaper. Most recently, she's opened an online boutique where she offers curated items from favorite designers in addition to a branded line of jewelry. I'd been following her for a few years and was thrilled to get the chance to interview her about her anonymous exploits.

> This whole silly experiment was born out of one night of actual coke talk with my friends back in 2009. At the time, I didn't know I was creating a personal brand. That grew organically over the following year. People started sending in questions, and I answered them. It was all party girl stuff at first, but eventually, my personal blog branched off into a full-fledged advice blog on everything from beauty tips to existential crisis management. It was great.

Coke Talk built a steady following throughout its first year. In the second half of 2010 she got an e-mail from Sasha Frere-Jones, who was building what would become the Arts section of the *Daily*, a bold new iPad-only newspaper. He asked if she'd be interested in writing a pseudonymous advice column, so Coke Talk decided to "level up and go pro." She contacted a close friend, an entertainment lawyer, who introduced her to an agent and helped put together a deal with the *Daily*.

By day Coke Talk works in entertainment and fashion, that's as specific as she'll get with me. She calls herself a "very private" person who chooses to blog pseudonymously in order to protect her career as well as the careers of those about which she writes. Her pseudonymity allows her to write honestly, not just about Hollywood debauchery, but intimate personal details. "It works because it's bullshit-free," she says, referring to the sort of equivocation that takes place when people speak while they're worried about how it might affect their quality of life down the road. This element of pure honesty is just as important to Coke Talk as privacy. She considers hedging based on reputational fallout to be poisonous to good writing. Anonymity facilitates creative honesty because it removes risk, which would otherwise motivate people to be fake in order to cover their asses.

It would seem that the only reason to publish anything under your own name, then, is because it provides reputational benefit which could lead to monetary benefit. And yet, here is Coke Talk, making a decent side income while remaining pseudonymous.

My persona has its own reputation, one that I continue to build. There's risk in that. When I started blogging, it was purely recreational, just a creative outlet. I never intended to get all professional with it, but that's what happened. So now, I'm in this interesting place where I have a reputation to protect, but it's not really mine.

She's always written, but this is the first time she's ever gotten paid to do it. She uses a lawyer and a couple of agents who know her real identity, and all business deals get funneled through a corporation she set up to keep her real name away from everything. In 2011, Coke Talk became The Coquette, which includes a style blog, boutique, and jewelry line that she launched with the money she saved up from writing her column for the *Daily*. "It's all turned into this bizarre second career that no one in my day-to-day life knows I have," she says.

It's been a blast. I think the most effort I put into keeping my identity a secret was when Rich Tong, the former fashion director at Tumblr, invited me to be a part of their Fashion Week initiative. I flew out to New York with a bunch of other fashion bloggers and attended all the events and parties under an assumed name. My pseudonym's pseudonym had a pseudonym, and I managed to stay out of everyone's photographs. It was all so much ridiculous fun.

Coke Talk writes about a lifestyle that some might consider to be "alternative." Sex, drugs, rock and roll. Her frankness inspires a lot of fan mail.

> Thousands upon thousands of questions, comments, rants, pleas, and the occasional nut-job manifesto. It's amazing stuff. People really open up when they write to me. I'm anonymous, they're anonymous, and the button they push to send me a message says, "Be Vulnerable." I think that's liberating, somehow.

As for any attempt to lock down identity on the Web, Coke Talk is skeptical:

> I inherently distrust anything that's supposed to make me "feel" safe. That kind of thing always has a background radiation of authoritarianism. Then again, I don't care if assholes like Zuckerberg waste time and resources trying to eliminate anonymity on the Internet. It'll never happen, nor do I need to bother fighting it, because anonymity isn't an ideology. It's just a methodology. People trying to eliminate anonymity are the type who don't know the difference between strategy and tactics. Those are always the ones who lose the battle.

The Whistle-Blower

Committing to blunt honesty turned a blog into a career for Coke Talk, but for the anonymous tell-all lobbyist at *Wonkette*, a politics blog owned by Gawker Media, it threatened her job status and exposed her to a minefield of personal trash talk. When I reached out on my blog for input from anons and pseuds, Megan Carpentier was the first to reply. That's her real name, but for years she was known to many as the anonymous author of "Ask a Lobbyist." Carpentier spent four months blogging anonymously for *Wonkette*, generating a fair amount of controversy, and attracting a wide readership with her insider's stories. Writing under an assumed name clued her in to widespread sexism, even within the so-called progressive blogosphere. She eventually came clean, resulting in the loss of several close friends, but she was able to parlay her experience into an editorship with Gawker Media and a full-blown writing career.

In 2006 Megan was working as a lobbyist. She'd graduated from college and eventually landed her dream job as a lobbyist in Washington, DC. But it wasn't what she'd imagined. Today she describes the experience as an "unending nightmare." Like many of her Beltway-bound colleagues, she read *Wonkette*. She'd been keeping up with their "Anonymous Hill Staffer," who was unceremoniously fired after being unmasked as the columnist at his own office. No one on the Hill wanted to see another Washingtonian scandal, in which a Hill staffer blogged about her illicit affairs (some of which she was paid for) with high-level federal employees.

Wonkette's editor, Alex Pareene, put out a call for a new columnist and Megan sent him an e-mail.

> I was emboldened by alcohol, seething hatred of my job, self-destructiveness and the fact that I had to write a weekly "humorous" recap of the week's events at the WTO. It probably wasn't that funny, looking back, but when you're that deep in the abyss . . .

Megan knew that outing herself and taking the job at *Wonkette* meant never lobbying again. And she knew that readers would balk at a new editor with no public writing experience taking a position as associate editor out of the blue. She felt like this would be a good transition out of a career she'd come to hate and into one that would be fresh and fun.

So began her stint as the anonymous author of "Ask a Lobbyist." Megan was careful about what she revealed and how she corresponded with Pareene (who didn't know her identity until after the column ended). Some of her readers automatically assumed she was a man due to her frank discussion of sex on the column.

Every third column or so, I'd try to answer a couple of the sex-related questions I got from readers. I'm not sure what exactly I said, but the tone of the comments was, effectively, no woman could possibly be so self-assured or blasé about sex, so this must be a man writing. And I only found out when my dad e-mailed me with the subject "I didn't know I had a son" and a link to the comment. So, I jumped in the thread to defend my honor, so to speak—I told them to call me stupid or venal, but not to call me a man, as that was just insulting.

She was taken aback by the idea that because she was a woman, she was supposed to not be interested in sex, comfortable with her body, or aware that other people wanted to have sex with her—and therefore, she must be a man. Furthermore, she was surprised that a bunch of self-identified liberal commenters on a liberal Web site thought that all women were automatically less confident in their sexuality.

On another occasion, Megan ignited a firestorm with a marijuana policy advocacy group by suggesting that the pot lobbyists enjoyed a little recreational drug use.

At some point, the reputational benefit of taking credit for her own work outweighed the benefits of anonymity. She knew that she didn't want to work in lobbying anymore, so she took the plunge and revealed her identity.

She immediately began to suffer the sort of ridicule common to smart female writers on the Internet.

It was . . . interesting? Most commenters were surprised, though it wasn't as though I was particularly well-known. Some made the inevitable "OMG she's fat! and ugly!" kinds of comments one would expect—including one who hosted a "poll" on his blog for his readers to vote as to which cartoon villain I most closely resembled, or if I was simply a trans woman.

Much of the vitriol came from her male fan base, who somehow felt tricked.

I'd get emails asking me out, asking me what I looked like, that sort of thing. . . . Given an utter blank slate and just my words on which to rely, some men had constructed—if the emails and nasty comments were any indication—pretty elaborate fantasies about how I looked, and had to a man all decided that I was seriously conventionally hot. . . . And I sort of expected some idiotic male disappointment that I didn't live up to certain male fantasies, though I did not expect the vitriol that came with being a boner-killer for those dudes . . . women are valued by their looks.

She says she lost several close friends after revealing her identity.

That some random dude on the Internet didn't want to gift me with his special, special penis and his personal stylings thereof was not what really fucked with my head. It was that people that I'd known for years, considered my friends, confided in, spent time with, accompanied to the hospital, cried with . . . that those people (a former co-worker, a friend in the biz that I'd know for years, people whose birthdays I'd celebrated and who had celebrated mine, that sort of thing) decided that they weren't my friends because of something like 70 columns and a career change, that cut me deeply.

But the outcry upon the revelation of her identity only served to convince Megan that she had serious writing talent, encouraging her to pursue further writing gigs with *Wonkette*, where she served as an editor, followed by editorships at *Jezebel* and a series of progressive news sites like *Talking Post Memo* and the *Raw Story*. She's come away from the experience with a healthy appreciation for anonymous discourse and is skeptical of any attempts to lock down identity on the Web.

There's plenty of commercial interest behind eliminating online anonymity, which makes me rather uneasy about any arguments made in its favor by those companies for whom it would be lucrative. But I also think that the very idea that discourse online would be made more civil by forcing people to use their real names is laughable to anyone that's gotten hate mail on the Internet from people's work accounts, from their obvious home email addresses, from people who will call you a nasty, ugly cunt who ought to be raped and die alone . . . with their sig file attached showing a phone number and address.

Megan stresses that persistent identity might force some people at the margins to be somewhat less horrific online, but if we recognize all the bullying that happens in high school, or the sexual harassment in the workplace, we find that identity does little to discourage abusive behavior. In many cases, having one's name attached to one's vitriol doesn't seem to correlate to consequences. Why should bullies expect any different online?

The Pickers

Not everyone turns to anonymity to make a big splash. Others just want to make an intimate connection with a like-minded stranger. When I put out a call for interviews, I was surprised to get a response from someone with dermatillomania, a condition I'd never heard of that deals with a habitual urge to pick at scabs. And then I got a second response from a second dermatillomania sufferer. The first had no connection with the second, so I talked to them both about their experiences with the condition and how they use pseudonymity to find strength and support on the Web. We'll call them "Bob" and "David."

Bob first found out about dermatillomania when he Googled it a few years ago, suspecting that he had some kind of condition, something more than just a bad habit that sometimes went embarrassingly too far. After finding a Web site about the condition, he learned that his compulsions were not his alone. He used the site to find a local therapist and started attending cognitive behavioral therapy sessions, which helped a lot. He still struggles with the condition, and he runs a Tumblr blog to connect with others who share it. He uses the platform to help other young people asking questions about the condition and provides support when he can.

David, on the other hand, is on Twitter, Tumblr, various forums, and chat rooms. He runs his Tumblr blog called *Diary of a Skin Picker* anonymously. His family and friends remain completely unaware of his dermatillomania, so he's careful about maintaining a divide between his online and off-line personae. He says that the Internet provides communities that allow him to feel comfortable discussing all kinds of issues, including "derm" in a way that they couldn't IRL. He initially started his Tumblr blog as a personal diary, and it eventually morphed into a support network. Over a hundred people follow David on Twitter.

Bob is over forty, he writes professionally about Silicon Valley tech, and anonymity helps alleviate the shame that goes along with derm, a condition often associated with younger women. He encourages his followers to seek therapy, which helps to legitimize derm as a real illness. David uses his platform to share his difficulties with his followers.

> I try to post what's really going on with me and not sugarcoat what it's like so that other people can feel like they genuinely relate. So I might say something about how hopeless I feel that day, or that I've just destroyed some skin or nails or lips, and I'll get responses from my followers full of support and reaching out to let me know I'm not alone. I try and do that for them too. It's a pretty supportive community.

David says that the stigma that surrounds skin picking would prevent them from ever being a part of a community built around discussing the illness, no matter how supportive. Although the community is supportive, and broader society has made great strides in accepting mental illness, admitting one's psychological issues will probably always be somewhat stigmatic.

Friends might become awkward, family might become intrusive, I don't even want to know how employers would factor this sort of thing in. Even strangers could call you out on it. Anyone can put their opinions out there. Someone you don't know could judge you for your illnesses and directly target you for them. Not your persona, not your activism, not your account, but you, because there's no middle man without anonymity.

Bob agrees, and tells me that he sees trolls harassing skin pickers who've chosen to confess their habits on Tumblr. One day he'd like to write a book about his experiences, but it's a gradual process. As of this writing, he hasn't told anyone about his illness other than his wife. People suffering from derm likely never tell anyone because of the stigma and shame.

It's like an alcoholic. They would never admit to being an alcoholic while they are drinking, but after going through AA or getting sober somehow, it becomes easier to admit that you were an alcoholic. . . . Maybe years from now I can tell people. I've thought about writing a book about my condition and how to deal with it, but don't know how a writer can remain anonymous. I know it can be done (I'm a book author as well under my real name), but would want to make sure I am anonymous until I don't want to be anymore.

The Troll Researcher

While some utilize anonymity for therapy, others put on a mask simply to observe. Whitney Phillips studies trolls. And that's not something you do under your real name. She uses a myriad of pseudonyms to embed herself within troll culture on Facebook (yes, it's possible to fool Facebook's real name requirement), 4chan, and elsewhere. She's a fourth-year English Ph.D. student at the University of Oregon, working on her dissertation, which focuses on online trolling culture. She approaches her subject from an ethnographic and media/cultural studies perspectives.

She'd initially planned to write her dissertation on political humor, but in the run-up to the 2008 U.S. presidential election, she became aware of a certain kind of antagonism happening on political blogs and social networks, which she now recognizes as trolling. From there, she began to actively seek out places where trolls hang out, like 4chan, for instance, and eventually Facebook and YouTube, as troll culture exploded into the mainstream.

Phillips says that trolls generally have multiple social media accounts, and they can pretty easily get around the measures taken by social networks to limit pseudonymous activity. She herself has dozens of accounts for Facebook alone, all of which were eventually banned, including her "real-life" account.

She's specifically interested in RIP trolling, a practice popularized by Anonymous, wherein trolls antagonize memorial pages set up by grieving families on social networks in order to pay tribute to someone who's recently been killed or committed suicide.

I think Facebook can do what it wants—they can try to restrict the behaviors, they can glorify "authenticity" in communication, they can establish all kinds of algorithmic tripwires, but that will only incite more trolling. They'll just go underground, hop platform, become more inclined to engage in kamikaze-style attacks. That's what has happened in the last year, when FB began cracking down on trolling behaviors in a much more systematic way.

As late as 2010, Phillips says that pseudonymous trolls could hang around on Facebook for months at a time before being banned. It's not entirely clear when Facebook began deploying algorithms designed to detect trollish behaviors, but it has become increasingly difficult for trolls to maintain persistent profiles, so instead they simply create new ones, change tactics, or go somewhere else for a while. Some trolls jumped ship during such "trollercausts" to alternative platforms like YouTube. As Facebook became faster and more sophisticated, trolls managed to keep apace in order to circumvent emerging security measures in the troll crackdown.

> Ironically, the harder Facebook made it for trolls to use the site socially, the worse/more vicious the trolling became. Because trolls were no longer trolling as their persistent troll selves, they were trolling under sock-puppet throw-aways. So the focus became "fast and dirty" raids as opposed to more drawn-out campaigns.

In other words, Facebook's push for persistent identity made the trolling problem worse. This reasoning can be applied to the broader Web as well, since it's more difficult to authenticate. Phillips dismisses the concept of authentication.

> First of all, "authentic" user anything is a weird and highly problematic concept. It assumes that "authenticity" isn't just possible but is the ideal mode of being online. More importantly, Facebook's model, and models that fetishize "authentic" identity generally, presumes/universalizes a kind of safe, middle-class sub/urban life free of everything but the lowest-level social risk ("if I post this funny picture of Mitt Romney, will my Mormon cousin get mad at me?")—and doesn't take into account,

doesn't even acknowledge the possibility, that someone's "authentic identity" could be a political or interpersonal liability. Or an issue of physical safety.

Phillips argues that the push for persistent social identity assumes that all persistent social identities are created equal and that this assumption is predicated on political and social privilege.

I don't actually know what we should do about anonymity—but I do know that abolishing it, just because it does (at least can) have a very high social cost, is the ultimate example of throwing the baby out with the bathwater. Lawmakers need to understand that a blanket/universal solution doesn't exist, will only disrupt the free flow of information online.

The Pundit

Whereas Whitney used anonymity to hide in the shadows so she could act as an impartial observer, others use it as a safer soapbox. I found "islamoyankee" at My Name Is Me, a new Web site where people can proudly proclaim their identities as they see them, whether they're birth names or pseudonyms. Islamoyankee, a.k.a. Hussein Rashid, is featured on the site. He took on the moniker as a blogger after reading an article about two things the French hate: Americans and Muslims. Thus, islamoyankee. He currently serves as a faculty member at Hofstra University and serves as associate editor at Religion Dispatches.

Rashid grew up in the '80s, in the age of video arcades, where players would use a three-letter handle to mark their high scores. He was "Wiz." He took on the name "islamoyankee" later in life. His name, while perhaps exotic to Westerners, is quite common in the Arab world, so the pseudonym helps him to differentiate himself online.

Rashid says he's a different person in class than at a family gathering or a PTA meeting, constantly reinventing himself in context.

> In face-to-face interaction, it's easy to draw distinctions in personality. In the digital world, the word reigns supreme. My personality is reflected in my name. islamoyankee tells you what you'll get from me online. It telegraphs who I am in that context.

I asked Rashid if he's aware of many bloggers within the Arab world who write under pseudonyms out of concern for their personal safety.

> I know of many in the Arab and Iranian world. . . . I never ask about real names because I know lives are at stake. I could not bear that burden if I ever did something that would put someone else in jeopardy. The type of transparency Zuckerberg hopes to create is a true sign of privilege. It's not for most people. I like the fact the Zuckerberg wants us to be open about everything, but he won't do the same.

Then I asked him about Mark Zuckerberg's statement about backing up one's words with one's identity.

> I think there are two things that are being conflated. I stand by what I say and I believe everyone should. However, there is a difference between power and leverage. That's what politics is. When I have power and security, I will speak openly. That may or may not affect change. If I want to change, then lever-

age is more important. Sometimes that means I can't be open about what I say. Either messenger or message can be difficult for people. You work in coalitions. You work anonymously. The latter is really important if you have neither power nor security. I think privilege, in this instance, is where people see power and leverage as the same thing.

In Rashid's youth, he maintained control of his personal communication through phone calls and notes. Today's youth rely on texts. He argues that the technology changes, but the insularity of teenage life does not. Some level of privacy is integral to growing up and finding one's place in the world. Furthermore, Rashid views the ability to control one's identity as a basic human right.

It is the very essence of what it means to be *homo sapien*. How could Descartes speak truth, in cogito ergo sum, if our entire existence was not bound in our individuality?

The Mommy Blogger

Some use anonymity as a weapon; others use it as a shield. Andie writes about motherhood with a pseudonym that she's been using for the last four years. As a parent, she has to be perpetually aware of how her writing might affect the safety of her children. She also has to think about what will happen when those children grow old enough to Google their mother's name.

Her blog is called *Blue Milk*, a reference to a theory that breast-feeding mothers who consume alcohol will produce milk with a bluish hue, a theory she rejects as being a way to control and shame mothers who wish to have a social life outside of motherhood.

She's a writer by trade, and when she's being paid for it, she writes under her own name. But when it comes to blogging and online publishing, she uses a pseudonym.

> I have left plenty of crumbs though on the path and people can easily identify me from one direction or the other if they're so motivated. Maintaining some level of anonymity, however illusionary, probably still provides me with a sense of comfort in my blog writing and makes for more adventurous and interesting storytelling on my blog.

There are loads of pseudonymous bloggers who write about parenthood. It's just common sense. Andie explores more contentious elements of parenthood like sexuality, which can sometimes bring a lot of negative attention. Her pseudonym is a safeguard against danger, allowing her to share and collaborate with a rich community of voices. She says that mommy blogging is quite confessional, because it rebels against the judgmental voices surrounding motherhood. But as liberating as it can be, it still involves an element of risk.

> Mommy blogging is also about the domestic sphere, by definition it is intimate. Women seeking to write about this topic are taking a risk—society can be very reactionary about this stuff, too, mothers have lost custody of their children for doing their mothering or organizing their family in contradiction to conservative mainstream views on what constitutes "good families."

She also cites the concern for the existence of predatory adults. But for the most part, her desire for anonymity boils down to the need for self-expression without consequence. I asked her what she discusses on her blog that she couldn't under a pseudonym.

Your in-laws, your parents, your sex life, your political views, your arguments with your partner, the times you stuff-up as a parent, the things your children do that really annoy you, the things other people's children do that really annoy you—anything that you wouldn't want your worst enemy reading and talking about behind your back.

The Second Lifer

Most people use pseudonymity as a tool to hide their true identity. The next person I interviewed takes on an alternate persona in order to transcend the self—to be the person she truly sees herself as. "Gwyneth Llewelyn" was another My Name Is Me find. She was one of countless casualties of Facebook's ongoing pseudonym purge, and more than anyone I spoke with, she offered fascinating insight into the spiritual implications of selfhood, here understood through the lens of Buddhist philosophy. Much of her worldview is drawn from the experience of transcending the self through participating in the Second Life community, a virtual world that offers near-limitless customization and the ability to be whomever, or whatever, you want to be. She resides in her hometown of Lisbon, Portugal, where she's focused on her Ph.D., regarding artificial intelligence in virtual worlds. She's been using her pseudonym since 2004, when she first joined Second Life.

Llewelyn says she made a mint in the dot-com bubble and subsequently lost it all after a series of bad investments with some business partners who, as it turned out, did not have her best interests in mind. Even after she'd lost everything, these men harassed her online and off, eventually encouraging her to kill her online presence and even leave home. Only her parents and lawyers knew where she went. The idea of a "second life" sounded pretty attractive to her at that point.

She saw a review of Second Life on an Apple Web site, and she initially thought it was a game. Second Life was particularly attractive to her because she could play on her Mac and her partner on his PC. They set up accounts and soon found out that Second Life is much more than a game.

At the time, Second Life gave users a choice from among a set of fixed last names, which they thought would provide a pretext for socialization based on users belonging to the same "family." She picked "Llewelyn" because it was particularly un-pronounceable and chose another Welsh name, "Gwyneth," as her avatar's first name for the same reason.

> I specially appreciated how many pseudonymous people in SL could thrive without anyone needing to check on their credentials. That was an eye-opening moment for me: we're defined by what we say and what we do, not really by who our credentials say we are.

Llewelyn soon realized that reputation is built on trust, and that trust is developed by different mechanisms than she once thought. She brings up the example of eBay's reputation struc-ture. When you join eBay, you start with a clean slate; it doesn't matter if you have a long-standing reputation as a businessper-son in your local area. You're only as reliable as your transac-tional history on the site, which enables people to own and shape their reputation. Llewelyn says that in Portugal, there was a time when "knowing the right people" was imperative in order to get by, and not having a strong network of back-scratchers and string-pullers at hand could mean the difference between success and failure, whether it was starting a business or buying a home.

She found her alternate identity on Second Life to be a liberating, democratic prospect that leveled the playing field. In her previous life she'd hired some employees for the company for whom she'd worked. For the most part, these people were hired on the weight of their résumés. When she discovered Second Life, she wondered what a company would look like if she hired solely based on talent demonstrated online. Race, age, education, even years of experience would take a backseat to raw talent.

In 2007 she tested the idea by launching a graphic design company that would develop professional content for customers wishing to have a virtual presence within Second Life. She hired all the staff online and says she still doesn't know who her employees really are. However, after several dropped hints, she was surprised to find that the company had a middle-aged double-Ph.D. programmer from England working under a twenty-five-year-old girl somewhere "in the middle of nowhere."

Some might see this as unfair. Llewelyn sees it as a purer meritocracy. Why should people be compensated for anything other than their current abilities? Pseudonymity allowed her company to reward results, not reputation.

In our society, we give a huge importance to our names. This is because we immediately associate them to what we call our selves. In most cases, it's something that is granted to you—you're born with your name and cannot change. The name is so important that married women will often change their last name to their husband's to indicate a change in social status.

But online we relate to our pseudonyms differently. They embody the abilities we have. In a sense, it's a bit more like the original idea of trademark: that name implies certain skills, a certain reputation, what you can do, what you have done, and so forth. Because online you can sort of strip everything out which is unnecessary.

Llewelyn thinks that pseudonyms allow us to become "more ourselves than we already are," a phrase she admits is odd. She's argues that theories about the self were incomplete until the advent of the Internet, a platform that allows people to redefine themselves, unlimited by physicality chosen by evolution, often harshly. What if her character in Second Life is her true self, and the physical body she inhabits on earth is her avatar?

The technology is new but the philosophy is old, about twenty-six hundred years old. Llewelyn draws her idea of the Self from Buddhism, which posits that the Self is an artificial construct based on our ideas, which always change. Our selves shift depending on context in the real world. "So we wear masks all the time," she says.

These days, we're all bombarded with books, movies, ads showing how overwhelmingly important our bodies are, and spend trillions in a whole industry of body enhancements, from yoga classes to cosmetic surgery. So there is excessive importance being given to the "body." Now, Facebook, Google and all have this problem: people online have no "bodies." But the next best thing is a picture of that body!

Societies are built upon persistent identities because they provide a mechanism of control. She argues that Buddhism warned about giving too much attention to the physical self millennia ago. With the Web, we're seeing the first generation of people who are able to at least partially transcend their physicality, though Llewelyn says that advanced technology is not required for people to do so, merely mental training.

[On Second Life] we invent our "selves" there (assuming we want to do so, of course) and can interact that way—sometimes in a far more sane and rational way. And we just create our bodies out of nothing; even avatars with no recognizable form are usually accepted. Neither the "self" nor the "body" is truly important. But this is just something you cannot describe or tell other people about; it will just sound like gibberish because most people are unable to accept it. You truly have to experience it.

The Activist Turned Developer

So far we've met people who live in the relatively free West. Now we are introduced to a man who knows what it's like to be put behind bars for one's ideas. I found "The Dod" through My Name Is Me. He's an Israeli-born software developer living in Thailand. The Dod is one of his many pseudonyms, which he takes on and off like gloves. He's had some for years, others for only a day. He doesn't talk much about his activism but he does claim to have protested drug laws, occupation, and privacy intrusions. "Identity is not a must unless you're a dictator's minion," he declares, and peppers his communication with phrases like "none of your business" and "but that's personal."

The Dod calls his pseudonym his "official nickname." He employs a roster of other 'nyms that accomplish various ends. The Hebrew word *dod* means uncle. He is an uncle to eleven kids. Even though it's his official nickname, he says it's his least important, since he needs more far removed monikers to conduct activism.

[The Dod] is just comfy, since people associate it with my various accounts on the net, but it's something I could ditch in

30 seconds when I smell the heat around the corner. "The heat" is a bit problematic nowadays, because it's not a binary thing like one day the heat isn't there and then "they're after you." They are always after you. From ad companies to regimes.

He says he's been arrested a few times in Israel, a nation he criticizes for its punishment of various thought crimes, such as calling for boycotts against certain state projects. Now he codes from Thailand while working on various software projects that he hopes will enable people to conduct anonymous activism. He shows me Mingle, what he calls the first "asocial network." It's a chat room with a bit of anonymization built in. The target audience is mobile, tech-savvy activists like the Occupy Wall Street crowd—a large group of people who can meet face-to-face for authentication, but require anonymity when communicating across the Internet.

Once the prototype is finished, he plans to include a white-listing option. So, one could create a group called "sound team for tomorrow's demo," and send out communications to a specific group of approved recipients via encrypted e-mail or Bluetooth.

> The main idea is that Mingle itself doesn't know that I think this is the sound crew, and you got that list from me. This makes data mining harder. Not impossible, but harder is good. The trend that started with Web 2.0 and is now called social networking had business models for leveraging relationship graphs. Today, these technologies help decide who to torture first in Syria.

The Doctor

Anonymity might be closer to you than you realize. I met WhiteCoat through a mutual acquaintance who edits a medical trade magazine. He'd employed WhiteCoat as a writer for quite a long time, all the while unwittingly maintaining a friendship with his real-world alter ego. Kind of like *You've Got Mail*, but less romantic. WhiteCoat writes a pseudonymous blog at *Emergency Physicians Monthly*, a magazine for emergency medical technicians and paramedics. He sticks to his pseudonym primarily out of respect for his patients. Of course, he changes the facts and circumstances of his stories to protect their identities, but his pseudonymity adds an extra layer of security. He also wants to avoid attacks from people who don't like what he has to say.

He says that a large corporation once called for sanctions against him when he penned an article critical of the corporation, and he suspects such attacks would increase if his identity were revealed.

"I could handle the attacks, but if I don't have to go that route, then why bother?" he asks. I asked him if he knows of any other pseudonymous bloggers within the medical profession, and he rattled off several.

> Some of the most popular medical blogs are written by anonymous bloggers. Dr. Grumpy, ERStories. MDOD. StoryTellER, The Happy Hospitalist, Nurse K., Living Dead Nurse, Dr. Anonymous, Throckmorton's Other Signs, Orac. The list goes on.

WhiteCoat is aware of fellow bloggers who have stopped writing due to receiving pressure from their hospitals. One time he was nearly outed when a nurse saw him working on a post at work, but as of now, only his wife and a few close colleagues know his identity.

He suggests that those who would attempt to abolish anonymity lead by example. I asked WhiteCoat how he'd respond to the abolition of anonymity as proposed by Randi Zuckerberg.

I would invite Ms. Zuckerberg to lead by example. Publish all of her social contacts, e-mails, text messages, and tax records online for everyone to see. Those are all "statements" she has made. Put up or shut up. Those who advocate sweeping social changes are often the ones who are least willing to abide by those same changes. And if Ms. Zuckerberg thinks for a minute that the world won't build a better anony"mouse" to counter the "great reveal" mousetrap she envisions, then she severely underestimates the ingenuity of the human race.

Further Faces

And these are just a handful of examples, people who happened to reach out to express their need for anonymity or pseudonymity. This cluster of interviews is only scratching the surface. The following are representations of actual manifestations of anonymity that I came across in my research, that I did not have time to describe in detail. But I list them here so as to provide overwhelming support for the value of anonymity. Consider the following:

- The rape victim who needs to find support online without having to worry about someone from her social circle finding intimate details.
- The mental health patient who chronicles the gradual progression of his delusions so that he can retrace the steps into psychosis in an open and accepting environment that will help him separate reality from fantasy.
- The closeted homosexual teenager living in the American South, whose parents would disown him if they knew his secret, looking for a supportive environment to discuss the tension between what he wants to be and who he is.

- The female gamer, who plays under an androgynous pseudonym in order to shield herself from incessant catcalling, come-ons, and exclusion based on her gender.
- The transgendered comedian struggling to find her footing in the comedy scene who needs an outlet to express her fears that she will be exposed and persecuted when her audience finds out that she was once a man.
- The middle-aged man who's really, *really* into collecting dolls and doesn't want his coworkers to know.
- The teenage girl who would like to simply chat with her friends under her given name, but cannot due to an estranged father who has used the social Web to harass her family in the past.
- The ex-lover who wishes to work through her pain and hurt caused by a soured relationship while respecting the privacy of the man who left her.
- The feminist writer who deals daily with death threats and otherwise disturbing e-mails from an unwanted audience.
- The minor celebrity who just wants to browse the Internet in peace without having her fame attached to everything she does online.
- The young Christian man questioning his faith in various discussion groups, asking questions that would mark him as a heretic were he to ask them off-line.
- The whistle-blower exposing the misdeeds of his employer, an offense that would surely get him fired were he to attach his name.
- The man who was involved in a public scandal many years ago, who insists he was wrongly accused, who still bears a scarlet letter in his real life daily and was drawn to the Internet as a place of respite from an otherwise judgmental world.
- The man named "Mohammed" who just wants to play video games without being subjected to racial epithets every day.

- The woman who is looking for a new job but doesn't want to alert her current employer.
- The woman who was a victim of identity theft and doesn't want to give anyone the opportunity to take advantage of her again.
- The functioning heroin addict who stands to lose his job if his employer found out, who has turned to the Web for support.
- The researcher who wants to embed himself within a pseudonymous community.
- A man suffering from AIDS who doesn't want his kids to know yet.
- The man going through a divorce who seeks legal counsel online, revealing details about his case that could incriminate him in court.
- The lawyer who writes fan fiction, who would be humiliated if his clients discovered his frivolous hobby.
- The CEO who runs a far-left political blog under a pseudonym because many of his colleagues and potential clients would take issue with his political leanings.
- The social worker who uses a pseudonym on- and off-line in order to protect her personal life.
- The foster mom who uses Tumblr as the hub of a support group for other moms.
- The former sex worker who writes cathartic missives about her experiences in order to educate young women.
- The elementary school teacher who wants to attend parties without having to think about who might be photographing her with a drink in her hand.

Again, these are just some examples I've come across among the countless cases of pseudonymous or anonymous behavior online.

I would never argue that the ultimate answer for marginalized people is to hide from oppression always and forever. If it weren't for brave artists and activists who were willing to let their identities be known, perhaps J. K. Rowling would be writing under a male pseudonym today. Likewise, putting names and faces to victims of abuse can often be hugely beneficial in spurring on social reforms. However, for many people it is the appropriate tool for the situation, pragmatically speaking. People must be given the ability to choose. It is not for me, or for Mark Zuckerberg, to decide whether someone should feel empowered to own one's words on a public, global scale.

When considering the above scenarios, it becomes clear why the identity issue is more nuanced than privacy vs. security. The "I've done nothing wrong, I have nothing to hide," argument is so shortsighted, and yet I came across it frequently when explaining to family members and friends about the subject matter of my book. We must do what we can to preserve the right to anonymity, and the first step may be to affirm the variety of its socially valuable manifestations, if, and only if, we preserve the free and open environment that allows them to flourish.

11

The Case for Anonymity

If one would give me six lines written by the hand of the most honest man, I would find something in them to have him hanged.
                                                    —*Cardinal Richelieu*

ON NOVEMBER 16, 2011, I logged into Tumblr, my blogging platform of choice, only to find that all of the posts on my dashboard were censored by big gray bars blocking out all text and images. At first I thought the site had been hacked, but then I noticed a call to action. Tumblr was trying to incite their users to protest H.R. 3261, a.k.a. SOPA, the Stop Online Piracy Act, an either insidious or bungling (I can't decide) piece of legislation that would give service providers not just the ability but the responsibility to shut down Web sites at the DNS level if those sites were found to be illegally hosting copyrighted content.

In a follow-up post, Tumblr's Rachel Webber wrote:

> Yesterday we did a historic thing. We generated 87,834 phone calls to U.S. Representatives in a concerted effort to protect the Internet. Extraordinary. There's no doubt that we've been heard.

On January 18, 2012, Wikipedia, Reddit, and over seven thousand smaller sites coordinated a content and service blackout to protest the bill. Google collected 7 million signatures. Anonymous attacked the RIAA (Recording Industry Association of America), MPAA (Motion Picture Association of America), and a bunch of other entertainment companies supporting the bill.

By the end of January, the Internet had declared victory over SOPA, after its mastermind, House Judiciary Committee chairman Lamar Smith, issued a statement admitting that Congress may need to rethink their approach.

> I have heard from the critics and I take seriously their concerns regarding proposed legislation to address the problem of online piracy. It is clear that we need to revisit the approach on how best to address the problem of foreign thieves that steal and sell American inventions and products.

SOPA, were it passed, would have represented a fundamental shift in the way the government controls the Web. The legislation would give the Justice Department the authority to monitor and censor Web sites accused of hosting or enabling the sharing of copyright. The bills' supporters insisted that the bill was only meant to put an end to egregious copyright offenders (such as The Pirate Bay), but the language employed in the bills was so broad that many community sites that thrive on user-generated content have publicly opposed it.

SOPA might be dead, but that doesn't mean the fight is over. Senator Patrick Leahy is responsible for a similar bill that appeared earlier, PROTECT IP, designed to preserve the integrity of intellectual property. In Europe, activists are fighting the Anti-Counterfeiting Trade Agreement, or ACTA. It's a multinational treaty intended to establish international standards for IP enforcement. Like SOPA, ACTA would profoundly influence the way the Internet works, affecting freedom of expression, civil liberties, and free-market exchange. ACTA is particularly insidious because its discussion among legislators has been less transparent due to its multinational nature. The Obama administration repeatedly denied requests to make the ACTA text public due to national security concerns. California congressman Darrell Issa was later able to release the text to the public in March through the OPEN Act. It, along with SOPA, PIPA (PROTECT IP Act), and FISMA (Federal Information Security Management Act) can be viewed at KeepTheWebOpen.com.

You may be wondering what these copyright enforcement bills have to do with anonymity. Let's be clear: the problem here isn't the copyright issue. One could go on forever about how this will smother entrepreneurship in the tech industry because big companies like Google, let alone Web start-ups, won't be able to afford to hire moderators to continuously monitor their user content, let alone a team of lawyers to fight copyright claims. Recent statistics show that forty-eight hours of video content are uploaded to YouTube alone every *minute*. Can you imagine what it would cost to monitor that volume? The government will never be able to regulate piracy away, but that's an argument for a different book. Forget if any of these legislations *should* exceed, it's unlikely that they *could*. What concerns me is that this blunderbuss approach puts the U.S. government in a position of editorial control that we previously would have criticized China for allowing, only to expand the perpetual game of whac-a-mole that is the war on online piracy.

McAfee's Dave Marcus is also skeptical:

> Let's say you have a Web server farm that hosts a thousand
> different Web sites. Let's say you compromise and put your

illicit material on one site. Does that mean the whole server farm should be shut down? You get into some operationally challenging decisions. Just black-holing a Web site doesn't mean the content goes away, it just means the site goes away. Twenty minutes later it'll show up on a different site.

The potential for collateral damage of free speech is real and opens up the possibility of bad actors only needing to accuse a site of some minor copyright infringement in order to silence free expression that might be happening there. A government agency that has the power to shut down a site at the DNS level due to a copyright claim (a favorite tool of those wishing to squelch critical speech, as we've seen) will necessarily shape the way that government deals with privacy and the right to anonymous speech. Zimmermann, creator of PGP, is similarly derisive:

> I think that there's something grotesque about having the Internet turned upside down just for the entertainment industry. When you look at how much economic activity is driven by the Internet and compare it to that of the entertainment industry—the entertainment industry is not that big! It's a small part of it. For the entertainment industry to have this control over the Internet . . . it's like if the auto industry was assembling cars at the command of companies who manufacture FM radios. Imagine if the people who make FM radios had absolute control over where highways can be built, and dictate crashworthiness. It's perverse. This is an example of powerful lobbies purchasing legislation.

Whether it's SOPA, PIPA, ACTA, or any such acronym, it's safe to say that content companies aren't done fighting.

Meanwhile, in England, a joint parliamentary committee is pushing to force Web sites to censor their users' speech under penalty of law. The committee advocates a new system by which someone who feels they've been defamed on a Web site can file a takedown order with a court. If granted, the Web site will be forced to remove the comments. If the comments are made anonymously, the Web site is compelled to take them down immediately on receipt of a complaint or bear responsibility for the defamatory remarks.

On September 16, the *Chicago Tribune* ran an op-ed written by Peter Baugher entitled "Remove Anonymity in Attacks by Cyberbullies." The essay cries out for new legislation that will end "the absolute immunity enjoyed by online service providers," since few people have the financial resources or legal knowledge to combat anonymous bullying.

> At the request of a user, service providers should be required to give anonymous posters a firm choice: agree to reveal who they are (to accept responsibility for their posts in their own names) or their posts will be taken down. Challenged posts would be short-lived or the author's identity would be exposed, subjecting cyberbullies to social sanctions and legal remedies. By rebalancing consequences for anonymous online speech, the law will dissuade abuses without sacrificing the vitality of robust speech.

Interestingly, Baugher is the father of one Julia Allison, a young woman who became a notorious microcelebrity for her spat with New York gossip blog Gawker, which published a vicious piece about Allison's incessant self-promotion among blogerati. Allison desperately petitioned Gawker to remove the piece, which generated a whirlwind of confused media attention ("Who is this woman and why do we care about her?") and vitriolic rubbernecking comments from readers. She spent a year trying to persuade Gawker's Nick Denton to take down the piece. Baugher fought alongside her, issuing cease and desists to a few publications, eventually persuading Wordpress to take down one anonymous blog dedicated to ridiculing Allison's very public antics. So it's easy to see why Baugher would want to do away with anonymous speech.

On November 15, 2011, the *Telegraph* reported on the Government Communications Headquarters scoring a £385 million contract with the UK government in order to carry out a new cybersecurity initiative that would focus on banning criminals and cyberbullies from the Web.

> The Ministry of Justice and the Home Office will consider and scope the development of a new way of enforcing these orders, using "cyber-tags" which are triggered by the offender breaching the conditions that have been put on their Internet use, and which will automatically inform the police or probation service.

How the agency will know if a criminal is using the Internet remains to be seen. Microsoft's chief research and strategy officer, Craig Mundie, thinks he has a solution. He's advocating a scheme that's colloquially been called "driver's licenses for the Internet."

> If you want to drive a car you have to have a license to say that you are capable of driving a car, the car has to pass a test to say it is fit to drive and you have to have insurance.

So, here we are once again, looking at an authentication process for the Internet.

Meanwhile innumerable Web sites, specifically newspapers, have been all too happy to integrate Facebook Connect, a free service that allows Web sites to provide convenient comment-ing functionality to their readers that's tied to their Facebook profiles. Bidding good riddance to their old commenting soft-ware, these sites have embraced Facebook Connect, which does away with the often abusive and unwelcoming commenter culture that goes along with the allowance for anonymity.

On November 29, 2011, journalist Paul McMullan, a seven-year *News of the World* veteran, revealed what many think about privacy issues during a round of questioning regarding the recent phone hacks at News Corp.

> In 21 years of invading people's privacy I've never actually come across anyone who's been doing any good. Privacy is the space bad people need to do bad things in. . . . Privacy is evil; it brings out the worst qualities in people. . . . Privacy is for pedos . . . fundamentally nobody else needs it.

Most recently, the government of India has asked Google, Facebook, and other social Web sites to screen content in order to filter disparaging, inflammatory, or defamatory content before it goes live. This would work like commenting systems where a human moderator has to read your comment to make sure there's nothing nasty in it before it gets posted to the site. Every blog post. Every tweet. Top executives from Microsoft, Google, Yahoo!, and Facebook are scheduled to meet with India's telecommunications minister, Kapil Sibal, but they aren't allowed to talk to the media about any of it. This chilling excerpt from *New York Times* coverage illustrates the attitude toward content screening:

> About six weeks ago, Mr. Sibal called legal representatives from the top Internet service providers and Facebook into his New Delhi office, said one of the executives who was briefed on the meeting.

At the meeting, Mr. Sibal showed attendees a Facebook page that maligned the Congress Party's president, Sonia Gandhi. "This is unacceptable," he told attendees, the executive said, and he asked them to find a way to monitor what is posted on their sites.

It's likely that these tech companies will not bow to Indian politicians, but these leaders have already begun constructing apparati to monitor users independently.

Perhaps more alarming is a story regarding Sony's vision for the future: authenticated electricity. In February 2012, Sony announced that it was building a smarter power outlet, which will potentially be used to authenticate those who plug their devices in. This way coffee shops could charge their patrons for powering their laptops or charging their phones. It also provides for an infrastructure that could allow for the widespread use of electric cars. It can also be used to manage the power grid, so necessary devices like medical equipment at the nearby hospital would be given priority over your video game console in the event of a power shortage.

The technology is a long way from commercial release, but we must consider the implications for personal freedoms. Everything else covered in this book is moot if minority voices can be squelched because they are too afraid to charge their batteries.

What we are seeing is an all-out war on anonymity, and thus free speech, waged by a variety of armies with wildly diverse motivations, often for compelling reasons. Indignant fury swirls around the anonymity debate, as free-speech activists are likened to child pornographers and those who wish to further regulate the Web suffer accusations comparing them to despots. Meanwhile, the face of anonymity keeps popping up in increasingly unexpected places. A robust cast of characters from countless walks of life throughout the globe have risen up and donned the mask (Guy Fawkes or otherwise) to fight for freedom of anonymous expression. Some fight with words, some with mischief, still others with legislation and civil disobedience. I have no doubt that this fight will be the defining social issue of the coming decade.

Not that this battle is particularly new. As we've seen, the struggle for the freedom to speak anonymously goes back centuries, as far back as recorded media itself. At every point in this conflict throughout history, there have been those who insist that anonymity is too dangerous. That we must choose between anonymity and security.

As greater portions of our waking lives migrate to the Web, and as our "real-world" lives and our online lives continue to blur, the conversation becomes increasingly crucial. We are not simply fighting for freedom vs. security, we are fighting for the ownership of our selves. Those bits of data that Mark Zuckerberg wants to sell to advertisers are just as much a part of who you are as your flesh and blood.

And yet, we are content to give them away willingly. Of course, I'm no hard-liner. I've maintained a Facebook account for years. The convenience benefits seem to outweigh the cost of selling my identity. But! It's something that I've chosen to be mindful of. I would never argue that we should close down all our social media profiles. These can be valuable tools, but it's crucial to be aware of the risks involved.

There are a few privacy advocates who believe we should regulate the Internet to enforce controls that make sense. danah boyd, for instance, has argued that Facebook has become a social utility and, like other utilities, should be regulated. She figures that people feel that they "need" to be on Facebook for professional or personal reasons, mostly because "that's where everyone else is." If we don't like where Facebook is headed, should we be relegated to a ghetto outside the commons? Or should a governing body step in to make sure freedom and democracy are preserved within Zuckerberg's walled garden?

> People's language reflects that people are depending on Facebook just like they depended on the Internet a decade ago. Facebook may not be at the scale of the Internet (or the Internet at the scale of electricity), but that doesn't mean that it's not angling to be a utility or quickly becoming one. Don't forget: we spent how many years being told that the Internet wasn't a utility, wasn't a necessity . . . now we're spending what kind of money trying to get universal broadband out there without pissing off the monopolistic beasts because we like to pretend that choice and utility can sit easily together. And because we're afraid to regulate.

I don't agree. If Facebook makes you uncomfortable, fight their behavior with everything you have. Join and give to the Electronic Frontier Foundation. But if in the end, your favorite social network chooses to favor profits over privacy, you can always go somewhere else. It may come with some sacrifices, but sometimes that's the price we pay to take a stand. Plenty of people have made that choice and are living happy, productive lives. Maybe you think Facebook will never go away and will continue to deceive and abuse its users. This view is dangerously ignorant of how consumer demand dictates the life expectancy of these social networks in a free market. If Facebook continues to ignore users' needs, a new service will arise to meet demand. Don't believe me? Just ask Tom from MySpace.

One of my goals in writing this book is to empower the

average Internet user with the knowledge to fight the identity wars, whether by petitioning for the end to things like SOPA, or simply routing around bad legislation through technology like Tor. These battles can be won if we simply understand the stakes. But I don't think forcing companies to adhere to certain standards based on their popularity is the answer. Regulators often begin with the best intentions, but their well-meaning efforts often have frustrating, unintended consequences.

Google opened 2012 by announcing that they would be integrating data from all its services. This means that if you are logged into Google+, Google will attach the information it's gathered from your use of Google Maps, Gmail, YouTube, and more. Perhaps most unsettling is that data collected from use of the Google-owned mobile platform Android will also be merged. If you have an Android phone, there's not really an option to be logged out. This change in Google's privacy policy will bring about loads of small conveniences, some of which we might not even understand yet. But, there will be a privacy trade-off, and the only way to opt out is to stop using all Google services that require a log-in.

Facebook's Timeline became open to everyone on December 15, 2011. When I first enabled the feature, I was shocked at how much information the site had about my life. But what really made my jaw drop was the amount of content on there that I had willingly supplied and now found incredibly embarrassing. I spent the next three hours or so going through my timeline deleting stupid wall comments, flirtations with romantic interests, pictures of me hugging ex-girlfriends, and regrettable political statements. Yikes. Life changes a lot in five years, and I didn't want my twenty-two-year-old self following me around like a wraith. Which brings us to the first concern about social networks that exert control over our identities.

Unwanted Permanence

Say I'm fourteen years old and I'm in a restaurant and I jokingly shout to my friends that I want to assassinate President Obama. Stupid, but hey, I'm a teenager. Everyone in the establishment will stare at me aghast for a minute. Some might glare or give me a piece of their mind, but everyone will forget about it tomorrow. Or to pick an example that hits closer to home, let's say I'm eighteen and I set up a blog that features, among other things, sappy, rhapsodizing poetry about my girlfriend. But I do it under a pseudonym, so ten years later, I don't have to worry about digging up those unbelievably embarrassing posts.

Today's teenagers likely don't have that luxury, because they're likely writing these things on Facebook, where everything you say is saved and, technically, could one day come back to bite you in the ass. When young aspiring writers ask me about how they can get into writing, I tell them to start blogging every day, but to do so with a pseudonym, because everything they write will embarrass them in no more than five years. Do we really want to live in a world where everything we say and do can be traced back to us, such that it follows us around, eternally branding us like a scarlet letter? People change. People grow. Perhaps you think this is a good thing. Maybe when you were young and stupid you never experimented with pot, or had an abortion, or made a racist remark, or said anything mean to anyone ever. Let ye who is without sin . . .

Even if an organization claims clearly in their terms of service that they will not hand over your information to a third-party entity, who is to say that they might change their privacy policy next year, and by then it will be too late for you to redact any sensitive info? Who knows how society could evolve in the future, where the words you utter carelessly today could be used to destroy your reputation decades from now?

Misinterpreting Aggregated Information

Let's say you download Tor. The next day you buy some fertilizer. The day after that, you post a rant about the Federal Reserve inflating the money supply. Separately, these things don't mean much, but when pieced together, a bit of liberal inference can paint an alarming picture. These are the sorts of things that a surveilling agency could potentially be looking for if given the ability to glean information from your Facebook status updates, among other channels. Even if we assume that authority figures mean well, mistakes are made. Death row inmates are proven innocent decades into their sentences. Information is misinterpreted. The more information the government has at its disposal, the more likely they are to arrive at terrible conclusions.

When I spoke with him on the phone, Philip Zimmermann, the creator of PGP, seemed to look back at the times when he was only speaking out against government privacy intrusions as if they were the good old days. Now we have "Little Brother" in addition to Big Brother. Zimmermann isn't on Facebook, and a lot of his reservations seem to be based in a healthy fear of how surveillance technologies could be coupled with the Facebook platform, namely facial recognition. He argues that 9/11 created a massive policy drive, a sort of "Manhattan Project" for surveillance technology. He brings my attention to shockingly powerful cameras that can zoom in on someone's face in a crowd from the top of a building hundreds of yards away.

By hooking that up to something like Facebook, it's a terrible combination of technologies. This is going to have a huge effect. I don't know what we're going to do as a countermeasure.

Facebook could provide the government with a global database of faces that can be linked to security camera footage. I've tried to avoid using the word "Orwellian" throughout this book, but this is about as Orwellian as it gets. He shares a thought experiment about a big hotel. Imagine a camera at the entrance of a hotel that records everyone coming in and out. Maybe there's a married politician staying in one. Maybe a woman enters the hotel ten minutes after he does a few times. Coincidence? Who knows?

Having such detailed information at our fingertips sounds like it would enable us to better discern truth from fantasy, but human error is all around us, and more data can often just mean more room for mistakes—mistakes that can ruin lives. Zimmermann calls my attention to a recent case where a teacher was fired because she was spotted on Facebook holding a plastic cup that might have contained an alcoholic drink.

Technology has its place, but it only gets you so far. I can't encrypt my face. Encryption is the low-hanging fruit. We have one area where we have the mathematical tools to achieve certain goals, but that's just one part of the privacy picture. The other parts have to be addressed within the policy space.

LexisNexis offers a product called Accurint for Law Enforcement that mines public databases to dig up people's assets, marital history, and contact information. The Internal Revenue Service uses Facebook for evidence of tax evaders' whereabouts. Employers routinely scan social networks for prospective hires. Chances are there is already a lot of information about you floating around on the Web, and the easier it becomes to draw connections between your different online behaviors, the greater the likelihood of misinterpretations.

Data Theft

The number of data security breaches in the private sector has increased by 58 percent year-on-year according to the UK's Information Commissioner's Office. When Microsoft talks about developing a driver's license for the Internet, I think of South Korea, which had a similar system in place until recently, after the most damaging online security breach the country has ever seen. The real-name registration system was introduced in 2007 and required users to authenticate their posts on certain popular Web sites with their birth name and address. Hackers compromised 35 million user accounts in July 2011.

And you don't have to be a superhacker to gather enough info to make someone's life miserable. Just ask the innumerable women who are stalked and harassed by ex- and would-be lovers in real life through information the stalkers have gleaned from the Web.

Tyranny Creep

As we've seen, the American Founding Fathers recognized the value of individual control over one's words. Their enthusiasm for anonymous activism may not have been explicitly protected in the Constitution, but it resonates throughout the rhetoric of the Revolutionary era. A future where privacy could be threatened was so inconceivable to the framers that they didn't feel the need to address it on paper. Being able to control who heard your words was the default status.

Some privacy advocates, Ian Clarke of Freenet among them, are optimistic about our future, given that citizens now have increased powers of surveillance through mobile phones, for instance, and increasingly robust communication channels, like Twitter. This vision of the future was laid down by science fiction author David Brin. In his 1998 book *The Transparent Society*, he suggests that within high-tech societies with less privacy, authority figures lose the powers of secrecy they use to abuse citizens. In this view, the groups like WikiLeaks and Anonymous will rise up to combat tyranny.

The idea is enticing, and it certainly seems like we are living in an era of great power redistribution and decentralization. But as we've witnessed during Occupy Wall Street and its related protests, citizens may have cameras, but the cops still have the pepper spray. The ability to countersurveil will only go so far as the rest of the fabric of democracy allows it. It's only part of the tapestry of freedoms. I submit that we must ensure that citizen surveillance is shored up by the freedom to expose authority figures with anonymity.

Every oppressive regime, all the way back to the Holy Roman Empire's census, has used data harvesting as a tool to accumulate greater control. You can't control a populace you can't see. As the Roman Empire expanded, so did its need to keep tabs on the far-flung peoples they had conquered. We see this continuing in the modern world, in East Berlin, Russia, and China. Information gathering is always the first step. Not all state-sponsored data analysis is malicious, of course. But it can be problematic when a populace doesn't know how its data is being used. According to a recent study by Stanford University's Computer Security Laboratory, consumers are far less anonymous while browsing than they realize. The study found that registering an account with NBC shared a user's e-mail with seven other companies, and Home Depot shared user data with thirteen other companies.

If you've read this far, I hope I've convinced you that privacy is not the same thing as secrecy. Just because you don't want to leave your front door wide open while you sleep does not mean you have something to hide. Anonymity and freedom of speech are so closely intertwined as to be inseparable. The latter is meaningless without the safeguard of the former. Free speech isn't very free when it can get you thrown in prison or worse.

And yet, here we are, with social networks pushing us to maintain a single identity and a variety of forces trying to limit namelessness on the Web for a laundry list of reasons that generally boil down to safety. But when you talk to the *real* security experts (as opposed to the politicians and the CTOs), they will almost uniformly tell you that trying to force a persistent identity across the Web is a futile exercise that would only serve to suppress free expression, doing little to inhibit any bad actors hiding behind anonymity. People who want to hurt people online will *always* find a way.

When I asked McAfee's Dave Marcus about this, I could practically hear him shivering with disgust over the phone.

> Yuck. Anonymity and transparency are a choice. I think it's abhorrent to think that we're going to have a net one day that requires every comment to be traced . . . that's horrific. No, the need for people to be able to post anonymously has never been more important than it is now.

The manifestations of anonymity are wide. Let's not kid ourselves—upholding the right to anonymity means enabling the occasional prankster, and even the child pornographer and the assassin for hire. These are abhorrent side effects of the preservation of anonymous activism. But it's something advocates of anonymity must come to terms with if they're going to seriously engage with the opposition. Mitigating anonymity will only inspire these evildoers to find new ways to hide, while repressing those who speak truth to power.

No one can force Mark Zuckerberg to allow people to contribute pseudonymously on Facebook. He owns the playground. But as political activist Lawrence Lessig says, "The Code is the Law." There's a good chance that where Facebook goes, so goes the rest of the Web. It is not incumbent upon Zuckerberg and his ideological cohorts to show the benefits of forced persistent identity; he must prove that the benefits outweigh the costs. So make your voice heard. If Zuckerberg had reason to believe that people weren't happy with his company's treatment of identity, he just might change it. And if he doesn't, some enterprising kid in a concrete-walled dorm will materialize to fix things. But it won't happen if we don't recognize that we're headed in the wrong direction.

Yes, anonymity lets you be a different person, but it also allows you to be who you really are. That's precious. Let's not give it up without a fight.

BIBLIOGRAPHY

Books, Articles, Court Cases

Anderson, Nate. "Spy games: Inside the Convoluted Plot to Bring Down WikiLeaks." Ars Technica. Last modified February 2011. http:/ /arstechnica.com/tech-policy/news/2011/02/the-ridiculous-plan-to -attack-wikileaks.ars/.

Andrews, Lori. "Facebook Is Using You." *New York Times*. Last modified February 4, 2012. http://www.nytimes.com/2012/02/05/opinion/sunday /facebook-is-using-you.html?pagewanted=2&_r=3.

Anonymous, "Ruin Life Tactics." Last modified May 2011. http://partyvan .info/wiki/Ruin_Life_Tactics.

Assange, Julian. E-mail correspondence on Cypherpunk List. 1995– 2007. Hosted at http://cryptome.org/0001/assange-cpunks.htm and http://cryptome.org/wikileaks/wikileaks-leak.htm.

Baugher, Peter. "Remove Anonymity in Attacks by Cyberbullies." *Chicago Tribune*. Last modified September 16, 2011. http://articles .chicagotribune.com/2011-09-16/news/ct-oped-0916-cyberbullying -20110916_1_cyberbullies-posts-aol.

Bora, Kukil. "2011 in Review: Top Computer Hacks That Shook the World." *International Business Times*. Last modified November 26, 2011. http://www.ibtimes.com/articles/256344/20111126/2011-review -hacks-shook-world.htm#page1.

Bosker, Bianca. "Facebook's Randi Zuckerberg: Anonymity Online 'Has to Go Away.'" *Huffington Post Tech*. Last modified July 27, 2011. http://www.huffingtonpost.com/2011/07/27/randi-zuckerberg-anonymity-online_n_910892.html.

Bradshaw, Tim. "WikiLeaks Delays Launch of New Online System." *Financial Times*. Last modified November 28, 2011. http://www.ft.com/intl/cms/s/2/ecac5dfe-1792-11e1-b00e-00144feabdc0.html#axzz1f2npcB3N.

Brin, David. "World Cyberwar and the Inevitability of Radical Transparency." Metroactive. Last modified July 6, 2011. http://www.metroactive.com/features/transparent-society.html.

Brodkin, Jon. "Authenticated Electricity: Sony Power Outlets Will Charge You for Charging." *Ars Technica*. Last modified March 15, 2012. http://arstechnica.com/business/news/2012/03/authenticated-electricity-sony-power-outlets-will-charge-you-for-charging.ars.

Brown, Barrett. "OpCartel Proceeds." Last modified November 3, 2011. http://pastebin.com/XZRpjUZq.

Canning, Simon. "Call to End Anonymity in a Bid to Expose Online Ad Abuse." *The Australian*. Last modified November 14, 2011. http://www.theaustralian.com.au/media/call-to-end-anonymity-in-a-bid-to-expose-online-ad-abuse/story-e6frg996-1226193976945.

Captain, Sean. "The Real Role of Anonymous in Occupy Wall Street." *Fast Company*. Last modified October 17, 2011. http://www.fastcompany.com/1788397/the-real-role-of-anonymous-at-occupy-wall-street.

Cave, Damien. "It's Time for ICANN to Go." Salon. Last modified July 2, 2002. http://www.salon.com/2002/07/02/gilmore_2/.

Charman-Anderson, Suw. "Could Diaspora Ever Challenge Facebook and Google Plus?" Last modified November 14, 2011. http://www.firstpost.com/tech/could-diaspora-ever-challenge-facebook-and-google-plus-130802.html.

Chen, Adrien. "Elaborate Anonymous Sting Snags 190 Kiddie Porn Fans." Gawker. Last modified November 2, 2011. http://gawker.com/5855604/elaborate-anonymous-sting-snags-190-kiddie-porn-fans.

Disqus. "Pseudonyms Drive Communities." http://disqus.com/research/pseudonyms/.

Doe et al v. Reed, Washington Secretary of State, et al. Certiorari to the United States Court of Appeals for the Ninth Circuit. No. 09–559. Argued April 28, 2010–Decided June 24, 2010. http://www .supremecourt.gov/opinions/09pdf/09-559.pdf.

Dwyer, Jim. "Four Nerds and a Cry to Arms Against Facebook." *New York Times.* Last modified May 11, 2011. http://www.nytimes .com/2010/05/12/nyregion/12about.html.

Edwards, Jim. "Julia Allison's Campaign to Rewrite History Is Coming Along Nicely." *CBS MoneyWatch.* Last modified January 18, 2011. http://www.cbsnews.com/8301-505123_162-42747228/julia-allisons -campaign-to-rewrite-history-is-coming-along-nicely/.

Espiner, Tom. "Akamai: Cyber Spies Are Hiding Behind Anonymous." *ZD Net.* Last modified October 14, 2011. http://www.zdnet.co.uk /blogs/security-bullet-in-10000166/akamai-cyber-spies-are-hiding -behind-anonymous-10024573/.

Gallagher, Sean. "Anonymous 'Dimnet' Tries to Create Hedge Against DNS Censorship." *Ars Technica.* Last modified November 2011. http://arstechnica.com/tech-policy/news/2011/11/anonymous -bit-dimnet-tries-to-be-a-hedge-against-dns-censorship.ars?utm_source =rss&utm_medium=rss&utm_campaign=rss.

Glynn, Casey. "Cyber Expert Parry Aftab's N.J. Home Targeted in Hostage Hoax." CBS News. Last modified July 26, 2011. http://www .cbsnews.com/8301-504083_162-20083493-504083.html.

Grandoni, Dino. "Former News of the World Reporter: 'Privacy Is for Pedos.'" *The Atlantic Wire.* Last modified November 29, 2011. http://www.theatlanticwire.com/global/2011/11/former-news-world -reporter-privacy-pedos/45508/.

Grassmuck, Volker. "Don't Try to Control the Network Because It's Impossible Anyway." *IC Magazine,* NTT Publishing, December 1994. http://ddi.informatik.hu-berlin.de/~grassmuck/Texts/remailer .html.

Griffiths, Emma. "Web Sites 'Should Carry Libel Risk for Anonymous Posts.'" BBC News. Last modified October 20, 2011. http://www .bbc.co.uk/news/uk-politics-15364774.

Grima, Joseph. "Open Source Design 01: The Architects of Information." *Domus*. June 2011. http://www.domusWeb.it/en/interview/open-source-design-01-the-architects-of-information/.

Howard, Alex. "A Manhattan Project for Online Identity." O'Reilly Radar. Last modified May 4, 2011. http://radar.oreilly.com/2011/05/nstic-analysis-identity-privacy.html.

Hughes, Eric. "A Cypherpunk's Manifesto." Last modified March 9, 1993. http://www.activism.net/cypherpunk/manifesto.html.

Hyneman, Charles, and Donald Lutz. *American Political Writing During the Founding Era, 1760–1805. Vol. I.* Indianapolis, IN: Liberty Press, 1983.

Kazmi, Ayesha. "How Anonymous Emerged to Occupy Wall Street." *The Guardian*. Last modified September 26, 2011. http://www.guardian.co.uk/commentisfree/cifamerica/2011/sep/27/occupy-wall-street-anonymous.

Kiviat, Barbara. "Driver's Licenses for the Internet." Time Business. Last modified January 30, 2010. http://curiouscapitalist.blogs.time.com/2010/01/30/drivers-licenses-for-the-Internet/.

Knafo, Saki. "Anonymous Clashes with Its Adversaries at Hacker Conference." *Huffington Post Tech*. Last modified August 9, 2011. http://www.huffingtonpost.com/2011/08/09/anonymous-hackers_n_921724.html.

Lemos, Robert. "When LulzSec attacks: A survivor's story." CSO Security and Risk. Last modified June 10, 2011. http://www.csoonline.com/article/print/684093.

Lenhart, Amanda. " Bullying happens more often offline." Pew Internet. Last modified June 27, 2007. http://pewInternet.org/Reports/2007/Cyberbullying/1-Findings/08-Bullying-happens-more-often-offline.aspx.

Levy, Steven. "Crypto Rebels." *Wired*. May 1993. http://www.wired.com/wired/archive/1.02/crypto.rebels.html.

———. *Hackers: Heroes of the Computer Revolution—25th Anniversary Edition*. Sebastopol, CA: O'Reilly, 2010.

Lowenthal, Thomas. "Not Anonymous: Attack Reveals BitTorrent Users on Tor Network." *Ars Technica*. Last modified April 2011. http:/

/arstechnica.com/tech-policy/news/2011/04/not-anonymous-attack
-reveals-bittorrent-users-on-tor-network.ars.

Manne, Robert. "The Cypherpunk Revolutionary Julian Assange." *The Monthly*. March 2011. http://cryptome.org/0003/assange-manne.htm.

Masnick, Mike. "The Definitive Post on Why SOPA and Protect IP Are Bad, Bad Ideas." *Techdirt*. Last modified November 22, 2011. http://www.techdirt.com/articles/20111122/04254316872/definitive-post-why-sopa-protect-ip-are-bad-bad-ideas.shtml.

May, Timothy C. "The Cyphernomicon." Last modified 1994. http://www.cypherpunks.to/faq/cyphernomicron/cyphernomicon.html.

McCoppin, Robert. "Web Poster's Anonymity Preserved by Appellate Decision." Last modified November 26, 2011. http://www.chicagotribune.com/news/local/ct-met-Internet-comment-ruling-20111126,0,4573864.story.

McIntyre v. Ohio Elections Commission (93-986), 514 U.S. 334 (1995). http://www.law.cornell.edu/supct/html/93-986.ZO.html.

Melvin, Jasmin. "Web Sites Leak More Info Than Consumers Are Aware Of." Yahoo! News. Last modified October 11, 2011. http://news.yahoo.com/Websites-leak-more-consumers-aware-164816491.html.

Meyer, David. "Hackers Plan Space Satellites to Combat Censorship." BBC. Last modified January 4, 2012. http://www.bbc.co.uk/news/technology-16367042.

Moore, Alan, and David Lloyd. *V for Vendetta*. New York: DC Comics, 1989.

Mullan, John. *Anonymity*. Princeton, NJ: Princeton University Press, 2007.

NAACP v. Alabama ex rel. Patterson, 357 U.S. 449, 462 (1958).

Nakamoto, Satoshi. "Bitcoin: A Peer-to-Peer Electronic Cash System." http://www.bitcoin.org.

Nguyen, Anh. "Private Sector Data Breaches Up 58%." CIO Business Technology Leadership. Last modified October 26, 2011. http://www.cio.co.uk/news/3313548/private-sector-data-breaches-up-58-percent/.

Nouveau, Trent. "Anonymous at the Forefront of OccupyWallStreet Protests." *TG Daily*. Last modified October 17, 2011. http://www .tgdaily.com/security-features/59099-anonymous-at-the-forefront-of -occupywallstreet-protests.

Nuttall, Chris, and David Gelles. "Facebook Becomes Bigger Hit Than Google." *Financial Times*. Last modified March 17, 2010. http://www. ft.com/cms/s/2/67e89ae8-30f7-11df-b057-00144feabdc0.html #axzz1ZY8EH5M2.

Opsahl, Kurt. "Facebook's Eroding Privacy Policy: A Timeline." Electronic Frontier Foundation. Last modified April 28, 2010. https://www .eff.org/deeplinks/2010/04/facebook-timeline.

Paget, François. "The Rise and Fall of Anonymous." McAfee Labs. Last modified October 21, 2011. http://blogs.mcafee.com/mcafee-labs /the-rise-and-fall-of-anonymous

Popper, Ben. "Rep. Darrell Issa Opens Up Secretive Intellectual Property 'Treaty,' ACTA, to the Public." March 6, 2011. http://venturebeat .com/2012/03/06/darrell-issa-acta-secretive-madison-open-treaty.

Roberts, Hal, Ethan Zuckerman, Robert Faris, Jillian York, Jillian, and John Palfrey. "The Evolving Landscape of Internet Control." Berkman Center for Internet and Society. Harvard University. August 2011. http://cyber.law.harvard.edu/sites/cyber.law.harvard.edu/files /Evolving_Landscape_of_Internet_Control_3.pdf.

Roberts, Hal, Ethan Zuckerman, Jillian York, Robert Faris, and John Palfrey. "International Bloggers and Internet Control." Berkman Center for Internet and Society. Harvard Law. August 2011. http://cyber .law.harvard.edu/sites/cyber.law.harvard.edu/files/International _Bloggers_and_Internet_Control_0.pdf.

Rosenbaum, Ron. "Secrets of the Little Blue Box." *Esquire*. March 1971. http://www.lospadres.info/thorg/lbb.html.

Ross, Nick. "LulzSec Teams Up with Anonymous." ABC.net. Technology and Games. Last modified June 20, 2011. http://www.abc.net.au /technology/articles/2011/06/20/3248520.htm.

"S Korea Plans to Scrap Online Real-Name System." *China Daily*. Last modified August 11, 2011. http://www.chinadaily.com.cn/world /2011-08/11/content_13095102.htm.

Schwartz, Matthew J. "LulzSec Suspect Learns Even HideMyAss.com Has Limits." *Information Week*. Last modified September 27, 2011. http://www.informationweek.com/news/security/privacy/231602248.

Seabrook, John. "My First Flame." *The New Yorker*. June 6, 1994.

Solove, Daniel. "Why Privacy Matters Even If You Have 'Nothing to Hide.'" The Chronicle of Higher Education. Last modified May 15, 2011. http://chronicle.com/article/Why-Privacy-Matters-Even-if/127461/.

Storm, Darlene. "Army of Fake Social Media Friends to Promote Propaganda." *Computerworld*. Last modified February 22, 2011. http://blogs.computerworld.com/17852/army_of_fake_social_media _friends_to_promote_propaganda.

Timmons, Heather. "India Asks Google, Facebook to Screen User Content." Last modified December 5, 2011. http://india.blogs.nytimes .com/2011/12/05/india-asks-google-facebook-others-to-screen-user -content/.

Wagstaff, Keith. "Occupy the Internet: Protests Give Rise to DIY Data Networks." *Time Techland*. Last modified March 28, 2012. http://techland .time.com/2012/03/28/occupy-the-internet-protests-give-rise -to-diy-networks/.

Wallace, Benjamin. "The Rise and Fall of Bitcoin." *Wired*. Last modified November 23, 2011. http://www.wired.com/magazine/2011/11/mf _bitcoin/all/1.

Wallace, John, and Michael Green. "Anonymity, Democracy and Cyberspace." http://www.computorney.com/anonarticle.htm.

Wallace, Jonathan D. "Nameless in Cyberspace: Anonymity on the Internet." December 8, 1999. Cato Briefing Papers. Cato Institute. http://www.cato.org/pubs/briefs/bp54.pdf.

Williams, Christopher. "Criminals and Cyber Bullies to Be Banned from the Web." *The Telegraph*. Last modified November 25, 2011. http://www.telegraph.co.uk/technology/news/8915245/Criminals-and -cyber-bullies-to-be-banned-from-the-Web.html.

Winter, Jana. "Inside LulzSec, a Mastermind Turns on His Minions." March 6, 2012. Fox News. http://www.foxnews.com/scitech/2012/03 /06/exclusive-inside-lulzsec-mastermind-turns-on-his-minions/.

York, Jillian. "When Social Networks Become Tools of Oppression." Bloomberg. Last modified June 7, 2011. http://www.bloomberg.com/news/2011-06-07/when-social-networks-become-tools-of-oppression-jillian-c-york.html.

YouTube. "Anonymous Veracruz Copia." Last modified October 6, 2011. http://www.youtube.com/watch?v=3ZL0E1J7wOg.

Interviews

"Andie." Interview with the author. December 15, 2011.

boyd, danah. Interview with the author. November 22, 2011.

Carpentier, Megan. Interview with the author. December 7, 2011.

"Coke Talk." Interview with the author. December 13, 2011.

Cottrell, Lance. Interview with the author. December 8, 2011.

De Rosa, Anthony. Interview with the author. November 30, 2011.

"The Dod." Interview with the author. December 13, 2011.

Emick, Jennifer. Interview with the author. December 12, 2011.

"Gwyneth Llewelyn." Interview with the author. December 12, 2011.

Hijazi, Karim. Interview with the author. November 17, 2011.

Marcus, Dave. Interview with the author. November 22, 2011.

Mayer, Jonathan. Interview with the author. November 20, 2011.

Phillips, Whitney. Interview with the author. December 11, 2011.

Rashid, Hussein. Interview with the author. December 12, 2011.

Shapiro, Dmitry. Interview with the author. December 6, 2011.

Sharma, Parvez. Interview with the author. December 8, 2011.

"Skin Pick Guy" and "Dermatillomania Awareness." Interview with the author. November 14, 2011.

Terban, Scot. Interview with the author. November 5, 2011.

Vader, Jeroen. Interview with the author. November 16, 2011.

Wilder, Isaac. Interview with the author. March 29, 2012.

Wysopal, Chris. Interview with the author. December 9, 2011.

Zimmermann, Philip. Interview with the author. November 21, 2011.

INDEX